THE ART OF BEING YAY!

The OMG NSFW Memoir and Guide to Authentic Joy

~

A book by

AIDAN PARK

The Art of Being Yay!
OMG NSFW Guide to Authentic Joy

Author: Aidan Park
Editor: Crystal Charee
Copy Editor: Robin Ryan
Cover Design: Kenneth Lui and Mariana Lui
Book Layout: Mariana Lui

A book by: Aidan Park

All Rights Reserved
A book by: Aidan Park

ISBN: 978-1-64945-949-7

TheArtofBeingYay.com
AidanPark.com

Tami -

- DEDICATION -

To Michael.

Thank you for teaching me how to love deeply, live fully and leading me to discover my personal joy. You will always be my Solar Shark :-)

TABLE OF CONTENTS

Acknowledgments

This book would not be possible with without the love and nurturing of my mother and my grandmother. Their love, strength and care was the foundation on which my character could be developed and I am forever grateful for their dedication and hard work. Thank you so so much!

Along the way I have met friends who have offered support, love, inspiration, ideas, care and camaraderie in times of joy and sadness. You guys have no idea the crucial role that you have played in my life! Thanks to my cousin Andy (MJ) who has been one of my biggest cheerleaders Jana, Blake, Leah, Lea, Scott, Will, Tuesday, Marina, Colleen, Jamie, Erin, Nina, Corey, Erin, Shawn, Stephen, Ana, Regan, Emily, Nancy, Stephanie, Kate, Emily, Sandy and Bea Stotzer, The Safkens, Piper, Amanda, Jen, Sam, Cyrus, Omi, Patrick, Alexis, Jean, Cammy, Joseph... I could literally go on and on. I love you guys!

Special thanks to my mentors and people who took a chance on me and believed in me. The ones who took me under their wing all along the way of my journey and encouraged me to grow. Val Peppinger, thank you thank you for never giving up on me. You changed my life! Richard Nickol and Bobby Weinapple my first mentors, you guys set me on a whole new trajectory for my life and gave me confidence to believe in myself! Thank you. Ms. Ennette Morton, you were the catalyst for this book to start you are my superstar mentor. To April Eckfeld who inspired me to expand on the book and serve the world in a deeper way! Solveig McLaren, my spiritual teacher who put me on the fast track to self-discovery and holds a space for love. I will forever be grateful for your generosity. Thank you! Margaret Cho, you have been an inspiration to me since I saw you on TV for the first time in 1995! Thank you for being my friend, your kindness and generosity is greatly appreciated.

This book would absolutely not be possible with my superstar editor Crystal Charee. Where did you come from and how did you just fall on my lap like that? Oh yes.. that's right. It was Robin Ryan! Who was also my copy editor! Thank you so much! I am so grateful that you both joined me on this journey! Thank you for challenging me to get realer, deeper and also to give myself a damn break sometimes. Tesa Colvin, thank you so much for believing me so hard and teaching me how to start this. I'm gonna make good on taking you on that vacation too! Michel Chicoine you gave me so many great ideas for this book, including the title, the interactive format and overall support that made this book so much stronger. Thank you!

People on my team who believe in me! Lisa and Carlee, you guys are like family and seriously had more faith me than I had in myself. Meredith, I would be so lost without you... the Madonna kitchen. Yikes. So glad I could catch up to you! HA! Donna K, hands down my favorite "show biz" agent I have ever had! Ginni Kim for all the help with the legal stuff! Ken and Mariana Lui superstar designers/layout experts. Holy Moly did I luck out with you guys!

This section's weird but I have to say thanks to all of those teachers that I have never personally met, but have made an incredible impact on my life. You guys have no idea. Thank you for your books, thoughts, observations, seminars and Youtube videos! HA!

And of course, I have to acknowledge Michael Arthur James without whom I would not have learned the importance in the Art of Being Yay. I am sure you know how much I love and appreciate you. I used to ask you if you knew I loved you and you always had the same answer for me "You show me every day." Ditto to you my Mickey J :-)

Foreword by Margaret Cho

When I watch Aidan Park do comedy I think, "Do I have a son? How would I have forgotten that? My son is here. My son…"

This is probably my greatest achievement. I think a lot of myself and my career and my impact on society just because I am now seeing many wonderful artists who seem to have been born of my body and mind. I don't know how well I have done on my own as a singular entity, but when I see someone like Aidan, I realize that I am amazing.

What we are meant to do here, the meaning of life - at least as far as I can assess – is to inspire future generations to do good, be better, be right, be smart, improve everything, repeat. So I have done that, I think. I do it through Aidan. I do it through anyone being proud and excited about their otherness, their gayness, their Asian-ness, their everything.

I don't know if you can be proud without pain though. I don't think you can be funny without pain. Pain allows our coping mechanisms to flourish, to laugh it off, to find a way out. We suffer and we are also our own medicine, our own comfort. Finding what is funny through the terrible truth of the awfulness of life gives us purpose. It helps us return to the battlefield to fight another day.

I have birthed a soldier in Aidan. Enjoy him.

The Art of Being Yay!

How to Use This Book

Hi guys! For those of you who are looking for juicy tell-all… You are totally in the right place! As you will soon see my life is full of drama worthy of a Lifetime TV Movie! So if you are simply looking to be entertained kick back and read ahead!

However, if you are looking for an experience that will help you discover your personal and authentic joy, this book is also right for you! As you go through the chapters you will see I share stories from my personal life which provide examples of why and how I came to develop the tools and principles I advocate. You will also get to see how I applied those principles to my personal life and how it worked to help me become more joyful! At the end of each chapter there is a scannable QR code which will lead you to an entry on my website that will guide you on how you can apply the tools and principles that I address in each chapter to your personal life to bring you closer to your authentic joy!

For the best reader experience, I recommend reading the book all the way through once, then going back and flashing the QR codes for more information the lessons from each chapter! This is an interactive experience! Feel free to scan the code, go to the site and leave a comment on the blog page and share your personal experiences as it relates to the contents of the chapter and connect with others who may have similar thoughts.

Also, my website has a ton of videos, resources and content all aimed at helping you be your YAY-EST self.

We are all in this together! Let's all create a more YAY-FUL world. I am so excited to connect with you!

Introduction

Hi! My name is Aidan Park and I am your author! I cannot believe that I get to say I am an author, considering I totally got a D in Miss Archer's English class during sophomore year. To be fair, English is my second language. I was born in Korea. Don't freak out. South. South Korea. So, relax and come out from under the table. Welcome to, "The Art of Being YAY!"

You might be wondering, What the hell is, YAY? YAY is a set of tools and principles that I employ in order to generate an eagerness for living. Like SpongeBob SquarePants; I adore him! When I perform stand-up comedy shows, I often get told that my laugh sounds just like SpongeBob's. To which I like to respond, "Yes, I know! I kinda look like him too -- yellow." (This annoys some people.) Anyway, SpongeBob SquarePants may be delusional and overly enthusiastic at times, but I love him because he never sacrifices optimism for the sake of realism.

I am an expert on the Art of Being YAY. I am a consistently positive person. Because I'm tall and smile a lot, it reads as though I had a lot of love and milk growing up. However, I was not born to a pair of dentists in suburban Orange County. I did not have a private school education. I do not have a trust fund.

In Korea, I was raised by a single mother because my father had a separate, secret family. When I was nine years old, I was brought to the United States as an undocumented immigrant. After we got to the United States, my mother then moved, without me, halfway across the country where she was blackmailed into supporting a man through dentistry school, under threat of being reported to the INS. I lived in my grandmother's senior housing, secretly, so I had to be quiet. That's probably why I am so loud now.

On top of it all, I was gay, while my family was hardcore Christian. During my teen years, I was depressed and even attempted suicide a few times. Somewhere along the way I developed an eating disorder. After all that, I got into college, but could not go due to my undocumented status. I also could not get a job due my immigration status. So, I became an entrepreneur; selling sexual services on Craigslist. I retired from that job at age nineteen, when I contracted HIV.

Eventually, I gained footing in life. I fell in love with a man I lived with for five years. Michael James. We were truly, madly, deeply in love, like that Savage Garden song from the '90s. A true and unique romance of a lifetime. Which made it all the suckier when he got cancer and passed away. He literally ghosted me. Jerk.

I say all of this to make the point that a positive state of mind and optimism was not something that I stumbled into. My life would have been a whole lot easier if I could have just fallen in love with a nice Korean girl and bought a house in Silicon Valley. I make daily decisions to lean in a joyful direction. It isn't always easy.

When it comes to emotions, we as a society are often told to "toughen up," "suck it up," "endure," as if we were all athletes for the WWF. If you buckle down and get it done no matter how much pain you're in, you'll win parental love, cars, trophy wives, and mansions. We have been taught that it's virtuous to ignore our emotions. A virtuous person is not supposed to resent working two or three jobs. Are you tired? There's a pill for that! Overwhelmed? There's a pill for that! We train ourselves to fake it. The dazzling personality, the high level of confidence, the wonderful leadership qualities.

However, when we are overworked, tired, or in a negative emotional state, our best qualities are not available to us. Do you ever notice how funny you are when you are in a good mood? Yeah, try being that funny after coming home to an overflowing toilet. That would be overwhelming and disgusting for anyone. But your emotional management skills and your general level of happiness can mean the difference between viewing the overflowing toilet as an inconvenience to be dealt with, or just another example of what is going on with your life and why you just can't catch a break.

"Be friendly."

"Be nice."

"Be compassionate."

That's all great advice for correcting a symptom. When you are happy, all those great qualities just naturally show themselves. A positive attitude, optimism, sense of self-worth, and clarity are the best tools that you will have in moving in the direction you want to take your life. It is the shift in your mind that generates happiness, not the changing of the conditions in which you are living. Believe it or not, six months after Michael died, he didn't rise from the dead and I was still in a terrible financial position. Nothing major had changed for me except the way I looked at the world.

When I started making emotional well-being a priority, I was able to consistently and deliberately make choices that inspired positivity. As a result, I was happier! As a result of being happy, I was cool to be around. Then, the more that people started to notice my increased level of optimism and general well-being, more people wanted to be around me. This included employers, employees, dates, friends, children, dogs -- you name it! It makes so much sense, right? Because who doesn't want to hang out with someone who is fun, positive, and easy to get along with?

Before my journey into "The Art of Being Yay", I remember days when a downward spiral would be triggered by something as insignificant as a long line at Starbucks, or stepping in a puddle, or a telemarketer. Any inconvenience would deem the day, "A Bad Day." Then I'd spend the rest of the day looking for further evidence of Mercury being in retrograde.

Because of the depression I experienced when I was a teenager, I've always had an interest in psychology. When I wasn't able to go to college, I decided to educate myself. I am an avid student of Neuro-linguistic Programming, various communication techniques, have studied concepts of EST training, am well-read on various tools used in therapy, and am a certified Life Coach. I have read hundreds of books on the topic of growth and effectiveness.

In addition to my research in psychology, I have studied many topics on the subject of development and success including: How to use language to talk to people, how to manage time, how to set up systems for businesses, creating rapport, public speaking, conflict resolution, and on and on and on. After losing Michael and being forced to deal with my emotional well-being directly, it became apparent the "how-to" that beat every other "how-to" combined was the "how-to" of emotional well-being. There are a lot of books I highly recommend checking out in the Further Reading section at the end of this book and on my website. What I'm providing in this book is a compilation of my best coping strategies and practical application based on the trial and error of my personal experience.

Certainly what I am about to share with you is not a cure-all. The truth is, I am not always happy. A good mood 100% of the time is a sign of mental illness, as far as I'm concerned. I have moments when I feel lonely, sad, and depressed. I have days when I miss Michael, days when I have bad dates and drink too much and make bad decisions with men, days when I binge on cheesecake while watching television by myself, living my life vicariously through *The Real Housewives*.

My life isn't perfect. But I have developed a closer relationship with my emotions. I am moving in the direction that I want with my life. I feel good about myself. I am proud of who I have become and am excited about what is coming. The increase in my effectiveness around people, business, and pretty much any task at hand was a completely unexpected side effect of being YAY. I cannot believe how few adjustments I actually had to make to my habits of thought in order to earn massive gains in my happiness, which, as a result, greatly improved my effectiveness. Seriously, you could spend an entire year with a dating coach who will try to teach you how to, "lock him down," or you could try being happy for a few months and you would net better results.

Excited? You should be! Because, once again, YAY is the best tool that I have discovered for getting everything I want from a practical standpoint (money, friendships, relationships -- stuff). The magic that happened as I got steadily joyful was unbelievable. YAY is like a superpower. Access the YAY and everything else falls in line. Best of all, I am going to share with you tools on how you can access your personal YAY! I am not shy about using my personal life as an example of these tools in action. This book is chock full of laughs, fun, and lots of oversharing. Buckle up, and get ready for a ride!

Find out more about why your happiness should matter to you!

Flash the QR CODE below for a video message from Aidan!

The Art of Being Yay!

CHAPTER 1

The Importance of Hope

In the 1940's, my nine-year-old grandfather was so badly abused by my great-grandparents that he ran away from home. He joined a gang of gold-miners going on an expedition to China. Grandfather and the gang had to walk from South Korea, through North Korea, in order to make it to China. My grandfather was successful in finding gold, which he then carried all the way back to South Korea. They didn't even have shoes with arch support in the 1940s, so it was money well-earned, as far as I'm concerned!

Grandfather then purchased my 17-year-old grandmother with dowry. Grandmother was a beautiful woman, about 5'2," with strong cheekbones and an even stronger will. Grandmother also had a very tough childhood, but due more to poverty than abuse. As a result, she received a minimal education and could barely read by the time she married my grandfather.

But Grandma had a flare for entrepreneurship. She became a real estate developer for some of South Korea's wealthiest families. This was before HGTV was a thing.

Before colored TVs even. Back when all Korean women had to wear dresses in public; the real poofy ones!

Grandmother was physically incapable of lying or being tactful. As a woman forged by living through two different wars, abject poverty, and a no-frills Korean culture, she never saw tactfulness as a value. Imagine her shouting, "The Raiders are coming to pillage our beautiful village, so it would be of our advantage run, wouldn't you agree? Please and thank you!" Everyone would be dead by mid-sentence.

Grandfather was insecure about my grandmother's incredible business acumen and empowered nature. So, he started beating her. The worse he beat her, the more Grandmother resented him and the less tactful she became, pointing out his shortcomings as a provider and that she was the bigger earner. Which Grandfather responded to by beating her again. Which then she responded to by outright insulting him. On and on and on.

The world was different before Oprah. Before self-development and psychology were "a thing," people would just be expected to suck it up. Although I recognize the fact that violence was normalized at a young age for my grandfather, of course I feel more sympathy for my grandmother. I knew her better but also, I mean, given the situation, it's pretty easy to be more empathetic with her.

My grandparents moved to the United States together in 1992, at which point my grandmother told Grandpa that he would never lay a hand on her again. One day, he went to grab her by the hair. "Not in America!" she shouted. She grabbed a hairdryer and smacked Grandpa over his bald head. I witnessed this. The irony of seeing a bald man get hit over the head with a hair dryer after attempting to pull his wife's hair was funny in a real dark sort of way. Grandpa passed away in 1996, two years after my mother and I moved to the United States.

However, long before this, my mother, Hee Sook Park, was born on January 6, 1961 in South Korea. The youngest of five, my mother had an amazingly deep, sensitive, and artistic nature. My mother is/was also very beautiful. So beautiful, in fact, that she was an actress in Korea during the seventies and won several beauty competitions! My mom's characters died in every movie she was ever cast in. She's been shot, drowned, hung, tossed off buildings -- all before the age of 21.

However, she had health issues from a very young age. She would get sick often with a mysterious disease that would render her unable to move for weeks at a time. It was attributed to stress as it would flare up during difficult life events. Two years before I was born, in 1983, the Park family lost their fortune due to my grandfather's excessive gambling. (This is also how the entire Park family turned to religion, for solace.)

The loss of fortune exacerbated my mother's illness. In Korea in the 1980s, wealth was a must-have status for any budding starlet, so she was unable to continue to act in films. She went from lifelong privilege to working in a dingy restaurant and sleeping there at night because she had no place to go.

During this difficult period in her life, my mother met my father. He was a tall man, with somewhat messed up teeth. Father charmed Mother, wooed her, and promised her the world. He said that he worked in the United States and had to fly out for business often, so he disappeared for a few weeks at a time.

He proposed, she accepted, and soon got pregnant with me. During her pregnancy, she was blindsided by the discovery that my father had a whole other family on the other side of the country. All those days when he told her that he was in the United States for work, it turns out he was spending time with Family #1.

During the months following her discovery, my mother fell into a deep depression. Mom cried morning and night and could not get out of bed. Korea in the 1980s had a very strict class system so the fact that she was going to have a baby out of wedlock was looked down upon by the community. My mother's friends turned their backs on her, my grandparents expressed deep disappointment and shame, and my father, unable to face up to what he had done, ghosted her.

My mother does not go into detail about how painful this experience actually was, and I can only imagine how alone she must have felt when she lost everything, almost all at once. Her health, her love, her parents, her friends. She was alone.

My mother's ill health and sadness had a negative impact on her and me during the birthing process. I was born premature and weighed two-thirds of the weight of a normal baby at birth. My mother had to undergo an emergency C-Section. The doctor then told my mother that there was a chance that her baby could be dead upon arrival. Spoiler alert, I live! And so does my mom!

The hospital had so little faith that apparently they

didn't even bother to try to resuscitate me and this is where my mother got her fight back. She demanded that the doctors resuscitate me. She shouted at the doctors while they were literally still sewing her shut from the C-Section. How badass is that? If that is not love, I don't know what is! All of the other drama that had happened in her life up until that point did not matter. She fought for her baby and she won. When she finally got to hold me in her arms, she felt hope again. In that moment, she committed herself to building the absolute best life that she could, if not for her, for the sake of her baby.

Okay, so how dramatic was that story? I have to say I love this about the Korean people. We feel things deeply and we are committed to our passion. My mother is no different! Have you guys ever seen a Korean drama? When something bad happens in a Korean drama it is not unusual to find characters on their knees, in the middle of the road (always in public), loudly exclaiming, "Why, God, why?!" as they literally pound their chest over melancholy piano music. However, knowing who my mother is and how much she loves me today, I believe her sentiments to be 100% genuine. I am very lucky to have a mother who cares for me as deeply as she does.

I cannot stress how important hope is to someone's well-being. In my mother, the hope manifested itself into physical well-being. Like my grandmother, my mother always had a talent for sales, but my mother had a natural grace and likability. After I was born, she was able to find a job as a salesperson for a wellness company which specialized in oils created in a shark's liver! (My mother claims that it was this miracle compound that saved her life after a particularly devastating run-in with her condition triggered by high levels of stress.)

After having saved a good deal of money, my mother decided that purchasing a video store with a live-in attached to the store would be a great way for her to spend more time with her son, and allow her to make money. Ever the entrepreneur, my mother offered one free video rental for every two video rentals to each customer. She was hot, so the men loved her, and warm, so the women loved her. In the end, she out-shined and out-priced the competition.

Jung Video (the business came with the name and my mother never bothered to change it) also offered a delivery service. Me! I was so good with directions and so friendly with all the neighbors that oftentimes people would call in their video orders and I would make deliveries to them. Sometimes, they would even tip me! I was a social butterfly, so I loved popping over to the homes of all the neighborhood characters and studying how they lived. I found it fascinating when men who came to rent videos in ragged jeans and worn T-shirts lived in beautiful, fully decorated homes, while oftentimes, the flashiest dressers would be living under a shack somewhere with a TV hooked up to someone else's power. Between our deals, personalities, and service, we drove all the other video stores in the neighborhood out of business!

My mother and I had a relatively happy existence until, one day, when I was nine, I saw a kid in the neighborhood I was friends with. I ran up to him and said, "Hi!"

He turned away like he was angry or embarrassed. "I can't talk to you anymore."

"Why?"

"My dad says that you don't have a father and I should not play with you because that is why you act like THAT."

I realize now that I was always a flamboyant kid, but at the time, I was super confused. I ran home, crying, and told my mother what had happened.

My mother is a very proud woman and especially considering the ostracism she had gone through during her pregnancy, she was very disturbed. So disturbed in fact, my mother got up from the video store and walked straight over to the hardware store where this kid's dad worked, and confronted him in front of everyone. She had no hecks left to give. That's it! Done-zo. My mother has the patience of a saint, but make her mad and, oh boy, watch out! All I can say is that they must have had the chainsaws locked up in the back because it literally would have been The Korean Chainsaw Massacre. Ditto for all the other weapons, axes, machetes. My mother loves horror movies. She had lots of ideas. I would have loved to have been a fly on the wall in that confrontation.

She came home from the hardware store and announced, "Pack your bags. We are not living in Korea anymore. We are going to live with your grandparents in the United States, where they don't discriminate against single mothers!" Okay… that was probably a little bit optimistic but I will tell you still compared to how Korea is against single mothers… My mom was right. She had also had it with what she correctly perceived to be a sexist attitude against women (this was around 1994) and economic inequalities that would have almost certainly prevented me from receiving a higher education. When I found out I was moving to the United States, the first thing I thought was, "YAY! Maybe I will get to hang out with Whoopi Goldberg!" Sister Act was my favorite movie and I thought maybe I could join the choir of singing nuns!

So, we came to the United States. Only one problem; we had no green card. Since we couldn't enter the United States directly, we had to fly to Mexico from Korea, where it is easy to pass customs, then drive through the borders with IDs that were provided for us by the "immigration coordinators" The IDs were supposed to have photos of people who looked like us but they heavily relied on the stereotype that "all Asians look alike." They gave me the ID of a fourteen-year-old boy (I was nine) and they gave my mother the ID of a woman who was a hundred pounds heavier than her. No joke.

This was my first acting job. My mother had me lie down on the backseat of the car and pretend to be asleep so that the border guards wouldn't question me. Which, now that I think back on it, was ridiculous. What kind of narcoleptic fourteen-year-old boy sleeps on the backseat during a drive? Anyhow, I complied. My mom stuck out her stomach. What an actress. Then we got to the border and they waved us through without even a second glance. I guess all Asians do look alike indeed!

We arrived in San Francisco to live with my grandparents. Within two years of arriving, my grandfather passed away and my mom took a job in Boston. I was left to live with my grandmother, who, around the same time, was accepted into a government apartment for low-income seniors. Good thing, too, because we were broke! The apartment was a carpeted one bedroom. Warm and cozy and perfect for us to nest in. It is be where I called home for the next 12 years.

As wonderful and loving as my grandmother was, moving in with her in a country that I was not familiar with posed several issues. Big issues. Big Changes. First of all, Grandma's home was a government apartment for seniors where I was not legally allowed to live. So, I had to be quiet. Being quiet is probably not my strength. I can't do anything quietly. As I am typing this right now someone is banging on the wall asking me to type quieter. So, for most of my teenage years, I remember feeling stifled and often confused.

Second, we had very little money. Grandma received a meager stipend of around six hundred dollars a month from Social Security. Mom sometimes sent money, but she was trying to make ends meet in Boston. Also, soon after her relocation to the East Coast, my mom got a boyfriend. She worked during the day while he attended dental school on an Army scholarship. But my mom missed her family and tried to break up with him, planning to move back to San Francisco. He was against that idea. He threatened to report her to INS if she didn't stay in Boston and support him through dental school. Meanie. I hope he gets halitosis patients for the rest of his life.

Another problem was, Grandma did not speak any English, which posed a big problem because I didn't speak English either. That meant that whenever a piece of mail arrived, we would just stare at the envelope and shrug. "If it's that important, I am sure they would have sent someone," she'd say. She couldn't read permission slips, help with homework, tell me how to get to school or even teach me to read. Neither of us could decipher a report cart which was just as well because...

Problem four...I was flunking. To go from being a popular, top-of-the-class student in Korea, to being ostracized for not speaking English was not an easy transition. Frustrated, I started having emotional meltdowns at school. I put on a ton of weight and hit two hundred pounds by the time I was twelve years old. I could not concentrate. My teachers threatened to hold me back, believing that I belonged in special education. I don't blame them. Had this been post-2009, I most certainly would have been given some kind of ADHD medication.

Problem five was that I hit puberty around this time and it became abundantly clear that I was absolutely a homosexual. I was like twelve years old when Backstreet Boys came out and I developed feelings for Kevin (the tall one). He was the oldest one. What can I say? I have daddy issues. I always seem to go for the older guys! Actually I became quite boy crazy. I was obsessed with Gavin Rossdale from Bush. He just seemed so sexy in his unapologetic ownership of his own misery. Ooh! Also, strangely, the guy with the dreadlocks from KORN. Also the dude from Collective Soul. Any male in music videos really. Also, I really loved Alanis Morissette. So, yes. Definitely gay.

To make matters worse, my family was puritanical Baptist. Finding Christianity brought my family members comfort in their turbulent times, but for me, not so much. Baptists believe in the second coming of Christ, wherein Jesus will return and take all of the people who have accepted Jesus into their hearts to Heaven. Literally. Like a

Greyhound bus driver could be driving a bus and if Jesus "called," the driver would disappear into thin air and all of the people riding the bus would be totally screwed (unless some Sandra-Bullock-like figure were to hop into his place, a la "Speed").

I was always concerned about things like that, actually. Like, what if trapeze artists are in the middle of a performance? One artist lets go of their trapeze, twirls gracefully in the air, reaches for their partner -- and there's no one there....all of the children in the audience would witness a bloody, bloody death!

I was taught about this concept when I was seven years old. I saw a movie called, "A Thief in the Night." The whole world gets raptured and the people left behind have a second chance to accept Jesus as their Savior. And, if they do, they have to run away from people who want to mark them with "The Mark of The Devil," which guarantees an Eternity in Hell.

"A Thief in the Night" was so terrifying that every day from around seven to about twelve years old, I was convinced that if someone was ten minutes late picking me up from school, I had been left behind. I would wait and wait for someone to show up and plan out how I would escape The Mark of the Devil by living as a recluse in the mountains. Or, maybe I could be like the kid from, "The Jungle Book." I'd befriend a bear who would protect me from harm if I bribed him with bananas....

One of my few joys in middle school was, "The Golden Girls." The show is about four older women who live together in Miami. I would get out of school at 3:30 and run to the bus stop so I could get home as quickly as possible.

I'd make myself a meal and then settle in to watch back to back episodes on Lifetime TV. It was my daily solace.

I fell so hard in love with the show that I would record the episodes on VHS (this was before TiVo) in case it ever got cancelled. Little did I know that Golden Girls would still be running nearly twenty years later. Like, it is still on all the time. On like, every network that proclaims to be for either women or The Gays. I am convinced now it's gonna just keep running forever until the aliens take over and even then, once the extraterrestrials discover the show, they will run it and broadcast it to their planets.

In case you have been living under a rock and never heard of the show, allow me to introduce you to these amazing women. Dorothy is the smart, witty sarcastic one who is built like a tree. Sophia is Dorothy's mother. She is eighty-three years old and is a straight-talking, sassy, tough, and funny Sicilian. Rose is the naïve and borderline doofus of a woman with a heart of gold, and Blanche is the southern woman who loves the company of men. Naturally, Blanche is my favorite. Blanche, Rose, and Sophia are widows. Dorothy is a divorcee to a slime bag called Stan who cheated on her with an airline stewardess.

I think what struck me most about these women was their "okayness." Even as a twelve-year-old who could barely speak the English language, I was able to pick up that these women had each had a lot of pain in their lives but they had optimistic, can-do, go get 'em attitudes. They seemed happy to me. They seemed like they were having fun! Their wellness puzzled me. Even at twelve years old, I could not imagine losing a loved one and being able to carry on the way these women had. They seemed like they were moving forward with their lives, not in the way that ignored the pain of having lost their loved ones, but in a way that was acknowledging and honoring the pain of such loss but leaning in the direction of happiness.

I can now see what these characters had that kept them joyful. Hope. They exuded the nature of hopeful people. The women were coming up with new business ideas, going on dates, trying to improve their relationships with their family members, taking pride in how they looked. They were hopeful about their futures and this hope was the very thing that kept them going day after day even though they had been through some tough life events. Even though, as is often the case in sitcoms, it never quite seemed to work out for them.

I think the show represented hope to me. I felt that if I could study hard and be nice to people, maybe, one day I could have a home in which I would have friends and people who loved me! At the time, I came home from school every day to an empty apartment. I had moved to the United States from Korea, and without a proper grasp of the English language, I had a tough time making friends. I went from being a straight-A student in Korea to almost being held back from 4th and 5th grade. It was a tough time. The worst thing about this period of time was the hopelessness I felt. Except when I was watching "The Golden Girls."

Also, I was going through all of these things with no internet. That's right. I'm old. This was even before modem dial up. So really, I had no community. No Korean chat rooms I could pop into. No one to advocate gay rights for me via the internet. Nada. I experienced extreme hopelessness between the ages of nine and fifteen.

I had let my mom and grandma down. I was failing school and I was gay. How disappointed would they be? They would surely disown me. I had let God down. He is all good and mighty and no matter how badly things go, God is supposed to be on my side. If only I were not gay, He might still love me. I had let myself down. Why couldn't I make friends? Why am I so fat? Why can't I control my eating? What is wrong with me? Why do I have to be like this?

I felt like there was truly nothing to live for and I had absolutely nothing to offer the world. I would wake up in the mornings, glare at myself in the mirror, and say, "Ugh, you again." I prayed to God to make me straight, or just kill me. I fantasized about running away and being gay somewhere else but I stopped because I figured I was too fat for anyone to want me to be a part of their gay club. Besides, I couldn't communicate with anyone, anyhow.

I made the lamest suicide attempts. I was too scared to do anything extreme but I would take cold showers in the middle of winter and then stand on the balcony. I hoped to catch pneumonia or one of those diseases that kill people in the Korean Soap Operas. One time, I took seven aspirins. When I woke up in the morning, I realized I couldn't even kill myself correctly. That was hopelessness. It went on for six years.

Until...one day on a whim, I decided to audition for my high school musical. To back up, in my school, in order to satisfy gym requirements, I could choose between dance classes, traditional gym, or join the U.S. Army Junior Reserves Officers Training Corps (JROTC). I didn't choose dance because I didn't yet know I liked musicals and I didn't want to take traditional gym because I was afraid of having to shower with the other boys. I was ashamed of my body and my very small endowment (the only comparison I had was porn I had downloaded illegally on dial-up internet).

I opted for JROTC even though I had no interest in the Army and was an undocumented immigrant. Everyone who chose JROTC was there because they were trying to avoid gym class. I still think it's an odd choice for the Army to recruit kids to defend our country who will do anything to avoid physical activity. Anyway, every Wednesday, I was required to wear the Army uniform to school for "inspection." And the audition for the musical fell on a Wednesday.

I was the only kid at the audition in a JROTC uniform, but I gave it my all. I sang, "Holiday" by Madonna. I don't know why I chose that song -- it sounded festive? I belted the notes the best I could and bulldozed through my nervousness by doubling down on gusto! Before I knew it the audition was over, and shockingly, I was not yanked off the stage with a cane. I thought, success!

Then there was the acting portion of the audition -- I could not read. I was 14 and didn't really learn to read English until I was 11, so I had to read the script for the audition and literally couldn't say the line, "OH CONDONE IT!" I think I said "OH CONDOOOON IT!" I kept interrupting my scene partner because I wasn't able to keep up the reading pace with how fast she was talking. I would either cut her off, thinking her speech was over, or just stare blankly at her until I realized it was my turn to say my line. The girl that I was reading with ultimately ended up with the role that she was reading for. That girl was a friggin' pro! Her manner toward me was reassuring, but she somehow still managed to stay in character.

I didn't have the reading comprehension to know what was happening. Were the characters on a date? Were they married? Were they Siamese twins? I didn't know and I didn't care. I was just worried about pronouncing "condone." Eventually, I came to learn that, "Where's Charley" is about some kid who had to get a chaperone to go on a date with a chick in the 1800s. He dresses like a woman in order to pretend like he's his own aunt. I didn't understand any of that. I didn't even know what a musical was. Why was everyone singing? What did "choreography" mean?

For the dance audition, I had to waltz. I was so nervous because I'd never held a woman before! Or a man! I'd never ever been so close to a human being. The dance audition was to a musical number called, "Pernambuco," and the first line was, "PERNAMBUCOOOOOOO UNBELIEVABLE TIME." Unbelievable time indeed. I stumbled through the audition the best I could. I could not remember the simple choreography. How did these people around me know what move came next? The choreographer kept saying, "1,2,3...1,2,3...." What was she talking about? What was this damn song about?

Miraculously, I was cast in the ensemble. I think the Art Department must have felt sorry for me, or saw something in me, or was impressed by my enthusiasm. It was all I had. The three women who put me in the play; Rita Dematteis, Nina Mayer, and Anne Vaaler (Drama, Dance, Voice, respectively) changed my life. I annoyed everyone in the play with my slow learning pace. I was off-key, couldn't say one line, and was pretty much just confused the whole time. I didn't even know what the play was about until we opened. I said, "Ohhh! Charley is the aunt? He dresses like a woman? Is he gay?" The other kids just rolled their eyes.

Being cast in the musical, however, gave me some self-confidence. Even though I wasn't good yet, for the first time in six years, I had found something that I had a spark of interest in. This spark gave me a reason to live and being part of the play made me feel like I belonged somewhere. Being cast in the musical gave me hope! I started feeling empowered again. I started to lose weight. I started to get better grades. I started caring about my own opinions and thoughts. I started taking care of myself and my feelings! All because I felt I had a reason to live again because I had something to live for. I had hope for something better.

Because I had been without hope for so long, my enthusiasm at the rediscovery of a possible passion was palpable. I became obsessed with the optimistic feeling that I had been without for so long. I felt good about myself for the first time in a very long time. I could breathe again.

In the four years following that fateful moment I was cast in my high school musical, I started discovering who I was. Due to the intense transition from hopelessness to hope, my excitement for life was double -- probably triple -- that of a normal student. During my high school years, I rediscovered my sense of humor, I found other gay friends in theatre who made me feel I wasn't completely alone. My skills in English grew exponentially, as I had to learn how to learn my lines for acting classes. I found my voice!

I also started reclaiming who I am. As my confidence

started developing, I started to question certain beliefs. Like does being gay mean that I am going to Hell? Does God really hate gay people? Are the Backstreet Boys really that much cuter than 'N Sync? I started to question why I had to be ashamed of my homosexuality at all! I am certain that I would not have chosen to be homosexual and was pretty sure that I was just kind of born this way. I mean Sister Act at age 6, really? Singing Nuns? C'MON!

I remember, specifically, the day I decided to stop giving a heck. All throughout middle school, I was bullied relentlessly for being and/or acting gay. Kids would usually say something like, "Hey, you are gay?" to which I would sheepishly respond…"No I am not."

One day, this kid who was notorious for giving me a hard time approached me to do what he loved to do best -- to make my life miserable. He was like 5'3," trying to project a "bad boy" image, so he had his own struggles. But he came up to me and said, "Hey, Faggot! You're gay and that isn't normal." Which is actually an odd insult. I mean, the statement starts with a derogatory name, but ends with an opinion rather than an insult. As a stand-up comedian, I see structural issues with this "roast," but I digress.

I do not know what came over me that day. I think the spirit of an angry drag queen that took over me. "Oh yeah? Being gay isn't normal?" I said. "That's not what your daddy said last night while he was sucking my dick!"

…Silence.

I could not believe I said this.

"What did you say?" he demanded. I braced myself for a punch or a tackle or something. "Cuz that was funny as heck!" he finished. And he gave me a friggin' high five. I could not believe it.

In the months after this confrontation, word got around that, "The gay kid came out of the closet and doesn't care." Then I started to get super popular. Unbelievably popular. It was probably helped by the fact that I was really good at these retorts.

This one girl used to make fun of me for being fat. (We're fine now. We are Instagram friends, so you know we are truly good.) Anyway, one time she said, "Aidan, hey, you have man titties!!"

"At least I got some, Miss Flapjack Pancake," I replied. This made her like me more, for some reason.

Then I just started not caring about anything. I started coming to school in pajamas because I didn't feel like changing in the morning. Then the kids would say, "That kid is so cool, he doesn't even care about dressing for school." I actually got a rolling suitcase because I didn't feel like going to my locker in between classes, and they thought that was cool too. It seemed that the less I cared, the more they liked me. Later, I learned the famous phrase, "The more you try, the more doubt you imply." Which is true.

I had re-prioritized my life to put the good opinions of others second to my doing, well basically, whatever I wanted to do. My passion and commitment to being true to myself in my own way worked for so well for me that by the end of my senior year I was elected not only the "Most Popular" in the yearbook poll but, OMG, this is cool, I was elected Prom Queen of my High School! Yes! Prom Queen! They also elected my friend Holly Dudiet as a Prom King!

A lesbian! We won! She is now a firefighter which is hella lesbian! I mean, she definitely has better luck with hoses than I do.

Hope and optimism are two of the most important tools you need in developing the skill of being YAY. Dostoyevsky said, "To live without hope is to cease to live." I know this to be true. Once I found a little something to live for (something as small as an ensemble role in a school play), it was enough hope to really change my life. My way out of hopelessness was gradual. Learning to superpower my happiness started with a sense of hope and a desire for growth. There is no stagnation. We grow or we perish.

Your hope and optimism matters a lot if you want a YAY-FUL life!

Flash the QR CODE below for more info!

CHAPTER 2

RAAS QUEEN!

College was something that I thought would be a given as I made it through high school. Once I got my groove back freshman year, I started applying myself seriously and I ended up getting serious in preparation for my future. I went to SAT prep classes, started studying harder to close the gap on my English skills, and somehow became part of a particularly high achieving clique in high school which consisted of me and three half-Asian girls! We are still very good friends to this day!

Colleen, sparky and intense standing at all of 5'1 was head of the debate team, a terrific student and a social activist who could never stand to watch anyone be marginalized. Erin was the valedictorian of our high school and played softball and golf, and totally not a lesbian. Marina was the heart of the group as she was president of Peer Resources and lead activism and conflict resolution seminars! At age fifteen! Marina taught me how to use "I-statements" to resolve conflict.

"I feel _____ when _____ because _____ and I need you

to _____."

I would often make fun of "I-statements" by saying things like, "I feel *bad*, when *you look at me* because *you are ugly* and I need you to *get a face lift or look the other way.*" Good Times! Marina is still the same. Last week she flew into LA from NY to go to a Non-Violent Communications seminar, which she invited me to attend along with her. It was so rewarding! I think the most important lesson that I learned was that, "Bitch, shut your punk ass up," is not effective communication.

These girls taught me what was appropriate in American culture. In Korea, when you see your friends, you say things like, "Wow, you look terrible. Maybe red is not your color." That translates as affection. No. Really. That is the Korean person's way of looking out for your best interests! A Korean person saying this believes that you have the potential to do better, which is a signal of care in the culture.

In contrast, Americans like to say nice things to each other even if they don't actually believe what they are saying. How is that helpful? Throughout my years of being in the United States, I found a balance between being honest and kind, so kudos to me! Instead of, "you look great!" or "you look like dog meat," I might say, "You are so beautiful. I know you can step it up and really dazzle in a different dress." I should write advertising copy!

Anyway, senior year, I was all set to go to college. My goal was to go to NYU where I could major in Musical Theatre. I could leave home, train in the arts, earn my own money doing what I loved, and meet more gay guys. I knew like two gay guys in high school (actually I knew like eight but six were still in the closet, so I didn't know!)

I had very kind drama teachers who really took care of me and wrote me some terrific letters of recommendation. Mr. John Propster, was a major player in my life in my junior and senior year of high school. He was a pleasantly plump hairy bear of a man with a heart of gold. He was a jolly but somewhat easily flustered drama teacher, who would often throw his hands up in the air and yell expletives but somehow managed to do it with love.

Ms. Nina Mayer was my dance teacher. She exuded grace and integrity with her powerful presence and clarity through her big brown eyes. If I had to elect one of my teachers for president, Miss Nina Mayer would be it. Cool, calm, collected, and honest. Ms. Mayer always believed in me through all my hysterics. She took me from not being able to touch my toes to being able to do splits both ways! When someone so consistent and steady believes in you and takes special interest in who you are, it without a doubt changes you.

I also was lucky enough to go to the American Conservatory Theatre for acting classes on scholarship where my lovely teacher Kate Brickley wrote me a recommendation of a lifetime. Kate Brickley was like Bette Midler and Diane Keaton rolled into one with a sensitive heart and a great gusto and passion that simply oozed from her pores. She was like my mama and I could just see her rooting for me with everything I did. I'm still Facebook friends with her, although I think she was hacked recently. I received a message about how she was lost in Cambodia and needed $2500 wired to her ASAP via Western Union, then she posted the following day about attending her daughter's graduation in San Francisco. What to believe?!? Any way you slice it, I was so blessed to have these wonderful teachers in my life.

After years of hard work in high school, I got great news! I had been chosen as one of the five students in our class of eight hundred to be a recipient of a scholarship to UC Berkeley! It was me and four other kids who all had like 4.5 GPAs. I was the fifth selection, even with a 3.5 GPA, due to my performance in Drama. I wrote my essays, I got my transcripts and turned in my forms...then...

I was called into the counseling office because I had chosen neither "resident" nor "citizen" on the scholarship application forms. I didn't have a green card and I was not a citizen so I just thought you could leave that part blank and move forward. I was told that in order to compete for the scholarship you needed to be a citizen or a resident of the United States. This meant that I was immediately disqualified. I was confused, upset and discouraged by the news but still felt hopeful I could attend perhaps with a loan or another financial support program. Unfortunately, I received even worse news soon after.

As I started getting letters of acceptance into various schools, I found out that I could not attend, because I was going to be charged international student rates even for community colleges, which ranged up to $100,000 a year or more in most cases! When I graduated from high school in 2003, there were no real protections in place for undocumented immigrants, and so there was no way for me to attend as a resident. I had no way to borrow the money to attend the school that I did get into. So it became inevitable that I would not be able to attend college right out of high school.

I was distraught but I thought, "Okay, I guess I will go get a job." I was so excited when I got my very first job offers; Noah's Bagels and Burger King! I thought, *I could take home all of the leftover burgers and/or bagels and feed all of my friends, forever!* Those big dreams were quickly dashed, also. Without a resident's social security number, I found out that I could not get hired. My dreams of becoming the best cashier at Burger King and wearing paper crowns while I worked were completely dashed.

After high school, I was completely stuck. No job. No school. And I was pissed. I had worked so hard in high school and felt I had been dealt another bad hand. I had studied hard, become a contributing member of society, and worked to better myself in all kinds of ways and here I was again. Helpless, hopeless, defeated. No matter what I did, I always ended up back in front of the TV, binging on cheesecake, trying to comfort myself with Lifetime TV and "The Golden Girls" reruns.

Hope or not, I needed something to do, so I took the next logical step. I became a Craigslist hooker. I couldn't get a traditional job so I figured, hey, why not get paid while having sex? I liked to do it for free, anyway....Plus, I had daddy issues, so all the guys I was sleeping with were old. Why not make a buck or two at the same time?

Standing on a street corner like Julia Roberts in "Pretty Woman" felt like too much exposure, so I made a post on Craigslist. The downside was that, unfortunately, the person hiring would be anonymous as well. If there was a fugly guy who approached Julia Roberts, she could run! Not so much with customers you meet from the internet, in dark alleys.

I met some interesting characters during this time. I was "hired" by a man named -- actually, I won't name him because it would ruin his political career. He was one of the most prolific anti-gay Supervisors in California and had built a career on the support of the socially conservative Latino base. He also worked in Immigration Law, so he was pro-immigration but anti-anything-gay. Supervisor was also extremely Catholic. I arrived at his house, and it was full of statues of Mother Mary. He told me to be quiet because his mother lived up stairs and he didn't want her to hear him have gay sex.

After each session, not kidding, he prayed. Which was convenient for him since he was still on his knees. Supervisor also had this habit of driving like a hundred miles per hour through city streets. When I asked him why he drove like that, he told me to relax because he had taken years of "defensive driving" courses. I'm not sure if he was showing off for me, or trying to get me out of his car quicker. While I was not attracted to him in the least bit, I think it gave me self-confidence to feel like I was desired enough that I had repeat customers.

Unfortunately, trying to fill my self-confidence with desires from other men was a never-ending black hole that just sucked and sucked. Ha. You see what I did there? At the same time I was getting paid for services rendered, I was also giving a lot away for free. I was running a not-for-profit and a for-profit at the same time. I was also not using protection or precaution.

Hope is paramount to well-being. The loss of hope and optimism for a desirable future put me in a dangerous state-of-mind. That's why I am so dedicated to optimism and hope. My attitude toward optimism can be read as naïve or uncool. I am not naïve. I just know that hope and optimism are essential to survival. I refuse to feed a pessimistic perspective in favor of looking clever or smart. Hopelessness is deadly. I am not theorizing. Hopelessness almost did me in.

Hopelessness led to my reckless behavior, which is how I became HIV positive at age nineteen. I initially took the test that came back as a "maybe." Then I went to get the confirmation test. I found out at a clinic, with my good friend Colleen. We went to Denny's afterwards and I binged on food. I think she took it worse than I did. I just kinda shut down and ate. All I remember is mozzarella sticks.

I know this story is getting pretty dark, but I would like to take a moment to point out that I am here writing this book and I am super-duper healthy and strong. So strong, in fact, that if you were in a room with me, and some maniac came in and threatened us with violence, I am so strong and fast that I can absolutely, positively guarantee that I would definitely beat you to the door and be out of the room, first. Bye, Felicia! So fast. Like Roadrunner. Sorry, Coyote, today is not your day!

Also, I am about to make a dark joke against the advice of everyone I have told this to, but screw it. I am a little bit annoyed because how can I get HIV, and then gain ten pounds? I thought being thin was supposed to be the only benefit, but instead here I am still trying to get off the last ten! For crying out loud. Is this joke tasteless? Probably. Do I think it's hilarious? Absolutely? Will the rest of the world think it's funny? Likely not. But it's my book and I am sticking to it!

Anyway, if I felt hopeless before, once I discovered I was HIV positive, I really, really felt hopeless. I thought I would be dead within two years. I grew up in the 1990s. In the 1990s, if a character in a movie found out he had HIV, he would be dead before the end of the movie. My feeling like I was going to die soon was not helped by the fact that when I would tell my friends I had HIV, the conversations would go something like this:

Me: I am HIV positive.

Friend: Are you okay? You are healthy, right? So you are not going to die...(fighting off hysterics) You. Are. Not. Going. To Die. (in full on hysterics) YOU CAN'T DIE, AIDAN! (on the floor, full-on extra) DON'T LEAVE MEEEEE!

Me: Um. There, there? I know...it must be difficult to find out your friend has HIV?

I have the propensity to become like a Kentucky housewife, due to my exposure to all those Lifetime TV Movies. I would say things in a southern drawl like, "We all have to go sometime, Hon!" or "When Jesus calls...."

But it wasn't even my health or dying that I was afraid of. I didn't even have the confidence to care about that. What was worse was the feeling of a terrible loneliness and hopelessness for my future. I thought that I would never ever find love, that I could never share this horrible secret with my family or many of my friends, that I would never be able to find anyone to truly love me or accept me.

Super depressed, I did what everyone does. I consulted Google: are people with HIV lonely? Short answer: yes. Quotes from lonely people with HIV. Sad posts from people who felt they had lost everything in their lives. Lonely people who had become reclusive and lived with their cats in shoe boxes. Homeless people making posts from libraries. People who lost lovers and friends and had been ostracized since the diagnosis. People who talked about how, "The Golden Girls" helped them through their lonely and difficult days. I thought, well good... as long as there is Lifetime TV I might be okay in my final years.

So at this point, I accepted that I would be lonely up until the day of my death. I then thought, *well just because I am going to be lonely doesn't mean that my life has to be completely sad. Maybe there are some famous people who died alone.* So I Googled: famous people who died alone. First result: Joan Crawford. Hmmm...well it's true no one really liked her but she did have fabulous skin. So maybe I would die lonely but I might die a lonely person with fabulous skin!

This went on for a few months, until the clinic where I had been diagnosed called to check up on me and suggested I go see the therapist they offered for free to the recently diagnosed. I thought, *What the hell...it's not like I am busy, since I can't be a Craigslist hooker anymore, or am busy having a job, or going to school. I may as well go bitch at someone.* That's what I thought therapy was. Neurotic people yelling at people who are paid to look like they are interested. So I wiped off my Joan-Crawford-inspired face mask and then went down to the mental health clinic.

I walked into a tiny room where a Marriage and Family Therapy (MFT) Intern was waiting for me. He looked too young to be a therapist and I could tell he was nervous, so I assumed he was an intern. I later had a boyfriend of eight years who was an MFT and he said the guy sounded like an intern, so let's just go with intern for right now. "Mark" turned on one of those white noise machines that are supposed to diffuse the sound so the people in the offices couldn't hear us. Little did he know, I was born with a megaphone built into the barrel of my chest, and was about to blow the building to smithereens with my anguish.

Dear, dear Mark got the full story. Everything. It was like an entire season of The Real Housewives, in twenty minutes. The "white noise machine" was not going to cut it. Seriously, people on Mercury could have heard my cries and screams of desperation. I am not delicate.

The theme of the session was, "I AM GONNA DIE ALONE (EXPLETIVE EXPLETIVE) I AM GONNA DIE ALONE (EXPLETIVE EXPLETIVE) I AM GONNA DIE ALONE (EXPLETIVE EXPLETIVE) THANK FOR GOD FOR THE GOLDEN GIRLS (EXPLETIVE EXPLETIVE)!" After I was done with my dynamo histrionics, I full-on expected Mark to sell me some bull crap about how, "everything is going to be fine" and "don't be so negative," blah blah blah.

Instead, Mark actually said something that changed my life. "You totally could die alone, Aidan."

Whoa. I felt such a rush of gratitude toward Mark. This was the first time someone had acknowledged the validity of my fears! Everyone else I had confided in had tried to shush my fears away. Their inability to face their own mortality led to them advising me to ignore my feelings. But Mark, by acknowledging my perspective, made me feel heard, validated and seen. I wasn't stupid or crazy. After all, Google agreed with me so I had to be somewhat correct, right?

Mark continued. "You could die alone, with HIV. But I just want to let you know…those two guys down the hall? The ones you met on the way in, are HIV positive. They have been HIV positive for twenty years and they have husbands, and one of them just got a house and the other one gave me a ride in his new car."

My first thought was, "OMG that one guy has a car in San Francisco? He's doing good!!" Then, out loud, I said, "Wait a minute. Google showed me so many people who have HIV, who are lonely."

"Yeah. There are people who die alone who have HIV but there are also lots of people who have HIV who live full, healthy lives!" Mark said. "They both exist… Just like people who don't have HIV. There are successful people who live full lives, and those who die alone and lonely."

I then thought…right… people do die alone without HIV all the time, as well. Joan Crawford didn't have HIV and she died alone. So…who is right? Google? Mark? What is the correct answer? I went home after that session confused. My assumption was that people with HIV die alone. Google said that they did. (I know, I know, this sounds dumb but I was nineteen and this was like beginning days of the internet when MySpace was the all the rage. Heck this was even before Friendster.)

So I went home. I Googled, "people with HIV who live good lives." And there it was! Hundreds and hundreds and hundreds of examples of people with HIV who live good lives. But just a few weeks ago, Google told me people with HIV die alone! Then I had a real AHA! moment. Google is a search engine. The results are determined by the question.

I had entered the Google world with some assumptions about the world of being HIV positive and I looked for evidence to strengthen those assumptions and proved I was right! Of course! I realized that I could find evidence to support any position or opinion about the world. People with HIV are not destined to die alone. The "dying alone" narrative was something that was perpetuated in some movies and became a stereotype.

So I had a choice as to which belief I wanted to feed:

1) Living with HIV will be a very lonely existence and you will have to keep this secret and face a life of solitude.

2) Many people have been diagnosed as HIV positive and lead wonderful lives with wonderful partners.

The only factual statement was that I had HIV. I could find evidence to support either potential belief, but one of those statements made me sad, and the other made me happy. I decided to feed the belief that was going to move me in the direction of hope, positivity, and optimism.

I started actively looking for people who had great lives who were HIV positive and I found a ton of them! I saw examples of HIV wellness through friends, in magazines, in group meetings, in dance classes, in books and TV and media. All of a sudden, they were everywhere. No joke.

Pretty soon, I was surrounded by so many people that lived with HIV who represented wellness that I started to believe wholeheartedly that living well with HIV was totally possible for me. This was not a perspective that I could have held before my meeting with Mark and now a whole new world was possible.

Over the years to come, I started to nerd out on

brain science. There is literally a part of the brain that helps filter out information that doesn't match our current belief systems. It's called the Reticular Activating System. RAS, Queen! Like, if you buy a new black Honda, you might see a lot more black Hondas on the road. It's not that there was a sudden increase in black Hondas on the road. It's the RAS in your brain that filters information and gives you information that is relevant to you. Isn't that crazy?

RAS works similarly on our beliefs. So, if you want to think the world is cruel, you can go out into the world and your brain will filter information that is discordant to that perspective and bring to you evidence of a cruel world. You'll notice someone being mean to a homeless person, or an angry driver flipping off an old lady. If you want to think the world is generally nice, your brain might filter out those experiences and help you focus more on someone giving a sandwich to a homeless person or a Girl Scout helping an old lady cross the street.

The world will provide the evidence for what you choose to believe. It's like The Matrix. (Side note: I have often been told I look like Keanu. I think I look like discount Keanu but that's also a belief so maybe I should stop saying that -- ha!)

Soon after my session with Mark, I returned to Google. I wanted to know if there were successful people who didn't finish college. Guess what? Thousands and thousands of successful people never ever went to college. Steve Jobs never finished college! Michael Dell of Dell computers never finished college! Anna Wintour (of The Devil Wears Prada) never finished college. Rachael Ray! No COLLEGE!

Okay, so what do I believe?

1) I can't go to college, so I will never get out of my grandmother's government apartment and will never find success.

2) There are lots of people who never went to college and found great success and maybe I can too.

The fact was that I couldn't go to college. Either belief about that fact could come true. I picked the one that was life-giving, not death-dealing. Life-giving perspectives are ones that move you in the direction of hope, optimism, empowerment, and strength. Death-dealing ones are pessimistic, hopeless, and dis-empowering.

I learned to be deliberate about my opinions because I realized that hope is necessary for growth and happiness. Pick the perspective that serves you best moving forward and find evidence that will strengthen you. You have more power than you think. Be deliberate! RASSS QUEEN, RASSS!!!

By the way, I am now an American citizen. I consider myself to be a great success and am surrounded by lots of love of friends and potential suitors. So. Do you think I chose the right perspective for myself at age nineteen? I am certain that had I chose the opposite perspective at that crucial time, my life would look a lot different for me now at age thirty-four. Special thanks to Mark The Intern, Lifetime TV, and The Almighty Google.

Choose Your Personal Truths Wisely!

Flash the QR code below a video message from Aidan.

CHAPTER 3

Success Mindset and Decision Theory

The discovery of successful people who had never finished college was huge for me! Again, I had found hope after a very dark time. When I learned about the possibility of success without a college education, I got so excited that instead of trying to figure out how to get into college, I started researching how the people who had not had a college education became the successful people that they were.

There was a common theme in the voices of all the successful people. They had simply decided that they were going to be successful individuals. Literally. They all kind of said, "I decided I wanted success and I learned how to do it." It sounded too simple to me. How does one just "decide to be successful"? After all, don't the personal circumstances come into play?

When I researched successful people on Google, I found a ton of information about each person. The person that I found most interesting was Bill Gates. Bill never finished college and is one of the wealthiest people in the world. Some people attribute Bill's success to his privilege. Lots of people attribute Bill's success to his talent. Some claim it was pure luck. Others claim it was Bill's undeniable physical beauty that led him to his successes.

Wait. No, now I am confusing him with Charlize Theron -- who is an incredible actress (and now producer) who became who she is because of what initially seemed like a major disappointment. Charlize originally wanted to a prima ballerina until an injury dashed her dreams and caused her to refocus her energies. Now she is one of the most powerful women in entertainment, who is not only an academy award winning actress, but more importantly a woman who creates and produces movies that brings light to important social issues. What a woman!

So, what are the factors of success? I instinctively took a look at which factors of success I could currently control in my given situation, and which I could not. Luck? What could I do about luck? Not much. Beauty? Sure I could work out and get a little cuter but I couldn't afford plastic surgeries or anything. Privilege? What could I do about that? Not much.

However, I did find other areas that his success was attributed to that I felt that I could actually have some control over. Bill Gates displayed tremendous levels of hard work. I could not control luck or beauty but I could certainly control how much hard work I put into something. Bill's mindset for success? I could learn that! Meeting the right people? Well...maybe not right away, but I could learn how to communicate better so I could be more comfortable around people. There was plenty that I had the opportunity to control within the suggested factors of success.

I threw myself into learning everything I could about

the mindset of success. I became dedicated to this art form for 16 solid years and will continue to be a student of it moving forward. Time and time again in all of the dozens of seminars and hundreds of books, the success factor pointed to two things; decide that you can do it, and focus on the elements you can control. I know it's so cheesy and so simple, right?

I am not saying this is a guaranteed route for success. Sometimes it doesn't work out exactly like as imagined. For example, I had dreams of being a superstar actor of stage and screen! In order to pursue my dream, I took like seven dance classes a week in exchange for cleaning toilets at Lines Ballet in San Francisco. I did work study for a generous but eccentric opera teacher named Richar Nickol who suggested that I buy a butt plug so I could practice an operatic breathing technique called, "butt to belly" which would compress my diaphragm and create a trumpet like sound effect that would make the entire building shake when I would sing (hint: it works). To strengthen my acting chops, I took it on myself to study Shakespeare, Ibsen, and classical plays. And I even toured with San Francisco Shakespeare Festival for a couple of years!

I found myself with some success in the world of acting and performing arts. I was in a good dozen commercials for products like Diet Coke (where I play a person who is not too happy about an eight o'clock meeting. My resting bitch face really paid off for this spot), Dell (where I play a straight geek who lands a really hot chick! (Actually it was Ariana from VanderPump Rules before she was famous! (she is very very nice and funny))). and the Kobe Bryant retirement commercial for Nike. (May he rest in peace.)

I also had a few bit parts in film and t and found some success in musical theatre. Okay full disclosure: success in musical theatre when you are an Asian guy means you end up doing nine productions of Miss Saigon. I did nine productions of Miss Saigon. That's right! I played the same character each time too! Thuy! The brutal Viet Cong leader because clearly I am so scary! Hey! I am scary. I am tall and can seem very imposing if you put me in a uniform and I am not moving or talking!

One time, I went to China to do Miss Saigon. Which means that the people from China had to fly to the United States to find a Korean to fly to China to play a Vietnamese person! Which I think makes me a multi-purpose Asian. I did some other productions other than Miss Saigon. I did Flower Drum Song once, where I played a dancing chopstick chasing a dancing box of Chinese take-out. I did it without complaining though. Cuz...I deliver.

In 2006, I was cast in a production of Ragtime. A week after I was cast, I was told that I was "too Asian" because the production team apparently thought that there were not many Asians in New York in the early 1900s.

"Are you gonna fire me?" I asked

"No, that would be racist...we will disguise you." So, no joke, they put me in a hat with Hasidic Jewish curls taped to the inside. I took one look at myself in the mirror and thought, *Wow, this is what the world's worst undercover agent feels like.*

One time, I was in a production of Hot Mikado. Hot Mikado was created by some sadistic individual who decided that a classical opera written in the 1920's would be excellent to adapt into jazzy tunes and sung in the style of R&B, ala Dreamgirls. Now, why would anybody do this? Presumably because they ran out methods of torture for prisoners of war and decided to do an experiment using non-union musical theatre performers.

I was cast in this production and was given ten days to learn the show. It was one of those shows where everyone was pretty much on stage the entire time. I will never forget the choreographer/director Samuel Carey who had to have been mainlining caffeine 24/7. He believed in us. By that, I mean he hired non-dancers and crammed complicated, head-achy choreography in every eight count so that there was constant movement and choreography happening at some corner of the stage at any given time. It was an ADD fantasy come to life. Oh, and then came the having to learn 7 part harmonies.

There was a point in the show where I literally had to do a split leap over three actors who were crouched down while I was singing a high B-flat (that's like, really high. Like if you had no balls, you'd still have trouble singing that high). To make things even more difficult, I had to listen for the cue and sing B-flat while six other people on stage were singing six different notes of harmonies that were apparently chosen at random.

One time, after a rehearsal, the director gave me a note to, "Try to look more natural. You look like you are struggling." No shit, I was struggling. Also the costume department put me in disco pants that were three sizes too small. I was sucking in so hard I thought my internal organs were gonna come out of my throat. My other favorite note was, "Aidan, try to butch it up a little." You know you are gay when you have to "butch it up" for musical theatre.

Every actor involved in the production cried at one point or another during the ten days. Every single cast member. Cried. Tears. You wonder why musical theatre people are "crazy." I think you would be too if you had to put up with this atrocity! But you know what makes me even crazier, is that I loved every minute of it. I got paid a handsome $275 a week for my work at Bucks County Playhouse that summer but I still remember it as some of the best moments of my life.

Okay, so the application of a successful mindset didn't turn me into an international superstar. However, I have to say I am damn proud of what I did achieve, and I had even more success applying these principles in the world of entrepreneurship. When I was twenty-five years old, I started working as a bubble guy for a children's party company.

Isn't that the perfect job for me? I am very bubbly. I am like walking bubbles! Sometimes, I drink too much and I am closer to sudsy, but I am bubbly. Also, have you ever heard of a gayer thing? I went to children's princess parties and made rainbow bubbles and put kids inside of bubbles! So, please, someone explain to me how a customer called Bubble HQ and told my boss that I was "too flamboyant" for their bubble party. Really? How gay was I that I was too flamboyant at this person's bubble party? Was it the sequined gowns? Was it the twerking? Unsure.

Joseph, my boss, was an amazing guy; a Frenchman who embodies the American dream. He came over and started a business and married a lawyer and has a cute kid.

One day, I suggested that he ought to expand his business up into the Bay Area so he could double his profits.

"Okay, Aidan," he said. "You lead the expansion."

It was rough going in the beginning. We had so many quirky employees who would flake. I would go to the Bay Area and teach people the scripts and how to make bubbles. Because we didn't initially have many customers, employees would quit left and right. Also, the Bay Area works differently than Los Angeles. In LA, everyone has multiple jobs as they pursue their real passion of working in the film/TV industry.

In SF, Everyone has to already have a full-time job in tech in order to barely squeak by. Only a select few artistic types in the Bay Area have the time and the personality to make great bubbles. Also, for this job you need a car to transport the bubble equipment. To find people who were good with children, could memorize scripts, had availability and a car in the Bay Area is like…well, finding an Asian in the early 1900s in New York. According to some musical theatre directors.

I did manage to find some people who were willing to work for us for a short time. Allow me to list a few:

Karl - A breakdancer who smoked a lot of pot. A lot lot lot of pot. He also refused to take off his beanie for bubble performances.

Sally - A clown-in-training who kept asking if she could wear a red nose to the parties.

Marie - A tiny girl who drove this monster truck who eventually had plans to relocate to Mexico with her mother to escape, "The Man."

Gerry - A former movie extra who said things like, "I worked with Robin Williams once and he handed me a clipboard and at that moment he looked at me and I knew that he believed in me...I could just see it in his eye. He was saying, "You got it, Kid!"

My favorite was Fannie. She and I are great friends to this day. Fannie is an Instagram model who would often leave me message like, "Aidan, I can't do the bubble show tomorrow because the bubble soap dries out my hands and I have to use my fingers to cover my areolas tomorrow for the photo shoot -- they cannot be dry during my nipple close-up."

"Okay, but can you do the afternoon bubble show?" I would reply.

When the business first started, I had to drive up to The Bay like three times a month to cover bubble shows left behind by flaky bubbleologists. Even my boss wanted to quit but I saw income potential there and I had decided the business was going to be successful.

People said things like, "it's based on luck" or "it's a tough market." But I had no control over either of those things, so I just focused on tightening up the training process, going to more marketing events, improving relationships with co-workers, and customer service. Because I could do something about those elements.

Four years later, we are a hit! I am so grateful to have found my stable team: Emery, an Energy Heater, Jason a full-on hippie from the '60s transported in time, enthusiastic Mallory who created an alter ego called MZ POP, Quirky Improv comedian and mother Alice, and, of course, sassy stand-up comedian Jess.

Another area of in which I applied a success mindset was with stand-up comedy. I produced a comedy show at a major comedy club in Hollywood and Long Beach for four years! It was an LGBT show called, "Rainbow Pop." Running a comedy show has its own challenges and rewards. For instance, once someone from the club office called and said something like, "We are shutting down the venue tomorrow due to fumigation, so we are moving you to the following day. That's cool right?" What? Huh?

Another time, it was, "All of your comics have been moved to the show next week due to a scheduling error, so I am going to give you a bunch of comedians who are not gay for your show but you still have to make sure the audience comes and has a good time." WHAT? But I just put on my RAS Queen hat and big boy pants and dealt with it!

One day, I received a phone call from the office five days prior to a show, saying that if we did not have at least 150 audience members, our show would be cancelled. My heart dropped. This email had come out to all of the producers at the comedy club. Half of the producers quit right then and there. I think I cried. I did not know how I was going to do this but I really didn't want to lose my show!

Then I remembered Decision Point Theory. Decision Point Theory is exactly what it sounds like. Making a decision and lining up behind it as to accomplish a goal. Simply put. Deciding. So I decided I was going to get 150 people. But, how?

Then I watched an episode of The Apprentice. This

was before Trump was President....I was a big fan of the show initially only because I could watch the fights and listen to the ridiculous things that celebrities would say as they were, "fighting for their charity." Celebrity contestants say stuff like, "Bitch I will cut you! In the name of St. Jude's Hospital!" I hate to say this, but I learned all of the business skills I know from practical application of concepts I learned from reality TV.

So when I was presented with the 150-seat challenge, I started mentally Rolodexing through what winning contestants of reality TV shows did to overcome crazy challenges. Then I remembered an episode where the contestants had to produce a circus in 24 hours and whoever sold more tickets would win the week's competition! This was Season 3, in which Kendra brilliantly monopolized the competition by approaching local businesses that were for children and offering them discount tickets and offered to raffle off items from their store at the circus and advertise them in exchange for an email blast to the clients. Brilliant. Just Brilliant.

So I gathered a bunch of flyers and approached every LGBT-themed business in West Hollywood. Which means I went to every business in West Hollywood. I visited drag bars, underwear stores, REI stores (for the lesbians), and even bathhouses (gay sex clubs) where they looked at me like I was crazy -- or they wanted to have their way with me. Whatever. Look at me however you want, just come to my damn show.

I hit my goal! So many people were at the show and I have to say this was one of my proudest achievements in my life. To make a decision to accomplish a goal, then to apply what I learned from reality TV to real life to make it happen. I have never ever been prouder of a business achievement. Kendra from Season 3 of The Apprentice, if you are reading this, thank you for your brilliant business savvy. You have no idea the influence you had on this particular viewer.

Decision Theory also might have allowed me to experience the love of my life. Look, I am quite a quirky guy! I have a penchant for coupons, the 99 Cents Only store, bargain-basement discounts, trashy reality TV, terrible '80's music videos, and I am a freak in the bedroom, with Daddy Issues! I was half sure that I was never going to meet the love of my life. Then 50+ Michael Arthur James walked through the door. Actually, I met him on a scuzzy, X-rated, gay hook-up website that shall go nameless, but who is counting?

We went on a couple of coffee dates before Michael asked if he could take me on a proper date. The only problem was, he was in between jobs. "Can I take you with a coupon?" he asked, sheepishly.

"Finally someone even cheaper than I am! Absolutely you can take me with a two-for-one coupon!" So off we went, to a very romantic restaurant. Some of you might know it. It's called HomeTown Buffet.

To meet a man who 20 years older than me who insisted he take me out for our first date to HomeTown Buffet with his 2-for-1 coupon, then thinking to combine those savings with his AARP card so we could both eat for five dollars. I was so charmed! Also when we got home, he had gifts for me -- stolen goods from the HomeTown Buffet. Gasp! I am talking forks and knives and Splenda packets. When I saw Splenda, I just died because there is only so much romance a person can take. After all, I am only a man. I told my mom what happened and she said, "You know it's true love when he is willing to commit a misdemeanor for you!"

We had great sex, too. Then, with the awful things that happened at my place, many of which I am sure are illegal in at least 10 states (complete with complaints from neighbors, etc.), I had met my match!

He would say, "I have been with thousands of guys and never been exclusive with anyone, but, Baby. You're it! That's it for me!"

I was like, "Thousands?"

And he said, "Baby, I am from New York."

The moment I knew he was the one, was when he sent me a video of a 70s artist named Lynn Anderson singing a song called, "I Beg Your Pardon, I Never Promised You a Rose Garden." Just the big hair on that woman. The big, big hair! She had this pastel green dress that you might imagine on a sisterwife of the 1920s.

One of my favorite things about Michael was that he had a hard exterior. He was a New Yorker, through and through. He would call out the idiots on the road, idiots in Los Angeles, idiots on TV, idiots in movies. But he was a big softie and anyone who knew him would agree. The thing I appreciated most about Michael was his emotional honesty and loyalty. You will never meet a more solid, surefooted man who acted with deliberateness and clarity.

Anyhow, despite the hard exterior that he tried to present, I loved his sensitivity and strong moral compass. I loved going with him to Dollar Movies to watch animated features. One time, we went to a movie called, "Sing." The plot was about a bunch of animals (pigs, gorillas, koalas, elephants, etc.) who were competing in an American-Idol-style competition. The koala, at one point, loses everything because his lizard assistant with one eye makes some kind of mistake that ends up burning the theatre down, and the cat who works for the IRS tries to take the property back.

When the koala stared sadly at the wreckage, Michael just bawled. His eyes kept tearing up due to his "allergies." I'd keep looking over at him and he'd say, "I've got something in my eye! Damn this moldy theatre!" He was even more sensitive than me!

"My sensitive Mikey!" I called him.

"Yeah. Yeah. Yeah… don't go telling anyone."

Whoops.

From an emotional standpoint, we were there for each other. I flew with him to Jacksonville Florida because his mother, whom he had not spoken to in ages, was found walking around her community, threatening people with a butter knife. He was so embarrassed to show me the community because he thought it was, "white trash."

"I think we got past that point when you took me to Hometown Buffet with your AARP card on our first date." I told him.

Anyway, we flew to Jacksonville and took care of her only for her to freak out on him and call him an asshole. But, regardless of what she did to him, he always took the high road and did the right thing. Even as he was calling her a "psychotic old coot" in his New Yorker fashion, he stood by her.

Michael made me funnier as a stand-up comedian. He came to support me at every single comedy show! He kind of acted like a stage dad. Michael had this gruff way of yelling at me, "I THOUGHT WE AGREED THAT WE WEREN'T GOING TO DO THE VEGAN JOKE UNTIL AFTER THE ROTTEN BANANA BIT! IT THROWS OFF YOUR RHYTHM!"

Sigh. Good times. In five years, we shared the romance of a lifetime. A trashy Harlequin novel complete with a house furnished with 99 Cents Only store decorations, a bucket full of sex toys, a Rolodex of characters, and Max, our beloved mascot and puppy. Michael moved in right away. We were like lesbians, from Day One!

I almost didn't experience the love of my life because of one minor hiccup at the beginning of our relationship. Michael had been a really successful real estate agent in New York right up until 2008, when the stock market crashed. Prior to 2008, he'd had seven properties purchased with unsecured loans totaling over eight million dollars! Then the bubble burst, and all of the sudden, no one was buying his properties. After about six months, the unfixed interest rates jumped from two percent to some crazy astronomical amount that Michael could not keep up with.

Michael tried in earnest to save his business and the homes, but he eventually lost his entire life savings. Then he moved to Hawaii in order to start fresh, but the stress of his loss caused him to have a heart attack. It took him close to a year to recover.

When I met Michael, he was almost eight million dollars in debt, and couldn't get a regular job because he had always been in real estate. I hooked him up with every connection I had. Sales, background work for TV and films, telemarketing. He never seemed able to keep any job for very long. I think it really hurt his ego to go from owning his multi-million dollar business to working for ten dollars an hour, asking people to subscribe to magazines.

At the time, this frustrated me, but in retrospect, Michael was right. He was not willing to tie himself to a menial job to merely eke out a living because he had dreams for something bigger. I think he intuitively knew that busying himself up with menial labor would sap the energy and focus he'd need in order to aim for something bigger.

I almost let him go because even though I loved every minute that I spent with him and we had such a great time, I had sworn to myself that I would never date a man who was unemployed. However, just thinking about breaking up with Michael (this was month three) brought me to Breakdown City. I mean it when I say Michael was truly the love of my life. For all his faults, he was the most loyal, loving, soulful, funny, kind, straightforward, and sexy man. Even at three months, I could not picture my life without him, so I sat down and did the math. I was about $1200 short on my monthly bills. I didn't want to sacrifice my lifestyle or Michael and so I decided to make the extra money and keep Michael in my life. This decision pushed me to think of creative ways to make money and created a new standard of living and income level for me moving forward.

I am no picnic to live with, either, and he overlooked and/or worked with me on all of my flaws. I am a messy guy who likes to keep his stuff scattered all over the place.

Michael always picked up after me. I had a bad habit of emotionally flying off the handle and Michael knew just how to calm me down. I could hold a grudge and make crazy leaps in logic. One time, I caught him smoking a cigarette after he told me he was quitting and I said to him, "Well, if you can hide this from me, you can certainly hide an affair. Can I ever trust you again?" I was definitely the psycho chick, but Michael loved me just the way I was and never ever demanded that I change for him.

The relationship got better and better. In the five years we were together, we were a power couple. Not only were we extremely happy at home, we started several little businesses together. We started a production company and shot a reality show (Aidan on the F-List), he helped me run my comedy shows at the comedy clubs, he encouraged me to approach the children's party company I worked for and pitch an idea for expansion to a new territory, and we also worked as political coordinators as we traveled up and down the state trying to get various propositions on ballots!

Michael had no problem working in general, he just didn't want to work for other people. But within the nucleus of our little companies, Michael was the paperwork guy. Hardworking and detail-oriented, Michael would come with me everywhere and while I led the charge in our entrepreneurial ventures, he would be the guy who kept it all together behind closed doors. The wind beneath my wings, as The Divine Miss M. would call it.

Making firm decisions that I could and would achieve my goals gifted me with surety and empowerment during challenges. So far in this book, I've covered three important elements in being YAY: Hope, RAS (manipulating our brain's stimuli filtering system), and success mindsets and Decision Point Theory. All of these concepts help explain human behavior, but it's being aware of them and consciously using them that allows us to provide an overall sense of well-being, even through the hard times.

And it's at this point in my story when I would need these tools the most. The five years I spent with Michael were some of the happiest of my life. I am grateful to him every day for who he was. But one day, Michael started to feel weak and his lymph nodes were suddenly severely enlarged.

Empower yourself with the success mindset!

Flash the QR code below for more info!

Chapter 4

The Demands of the Whiteboard

The three months after Michael's lymph nodes swelled up were a hellish nightmare. Once we went to the doctor, every step of the way, the news was the worst possible. It took an entire two months before we got the official word that it was cancer, and by then his condition had worsened so much that he was living in the ICU.

First, we went to the emergency room, where they told us Michael needed a biopsy. But the biopsy had to be done off-site by a biopsy specialist to see if it was cancer before they were able to treat him with any kind of chemotherapy. Biopsies were only able to be done once he was released from the emergency room. Apparently, emergency rooms were only for pain management and making sure he was well enough to...uhh...leave?

The insurance companies were no help. The biopsy had to be approved and two weeks after the trip to the emergency room, we got to meet the biopsy specialist who informed us that we needed an oncologist to sign off on the biopsy. He referred us over to an oncologist and we had to wait another two weeks for the insurance to approve the oncologist and for us to get an appointment.

While we were waiting for the medical community to catch up, Michael kept having to make trips to the emergency room for pain management issues. He needed oxycodone/norco and some heavy doses of painkillers to manage his discomfort, but the doctors would frequently under-prescribe, leading Michael to run out of pills. Also, the laws had limited pharmacies their distribution amounts due to the opioid crisis. Another problem was that pharmacies could not tell you via telephone whether they had met the maximum distributed or not. So, each day, I would drive to up to seven different pharmacies with prescriptions, praying that they had not hit their limit.

Also, often, I would be told that Michael's insurance could not cover the pills that we needed from the pharmacy and they would have to submit for approval which would take up to three days -- longer, if it was a weekend. So, we purchased the medication with credit cards. Michael and I used all of our savings and maxed out all our credit cards during those three short months. We had no time to wait for insurance companies.

I knew it was cancer even though we had not received the official diagnosis, and we were being jerked around by medical bureaucracy, so I applied the skills I had developed to saving Michael. I decided that the cancer was beatable. I researched the many people who miraculously beat cancer and decided Michael was going to be one of them. I also decided that Michael was going to beat cancer with or without the help of the medical community.

It sounds as though Michael had very little part in

the decision-making process, and that's true. He was on pain pills almost immediately. We were lucky if he could complete a sentence. I was so terrified of losing him that I would have chopped my arm right off and sold it in the black market if it meant that I could have any little bit of hope of having him healthy again.

As chopping my arm off would not have helped, instead, I found holistic cancer specialists, spoke to college professors with specialties in oncology who spoke about alternative methods for healing, consulted every healer I could get in touch with and, of course, I WebMD'd like crazy. I took the save-him-at-all-costs point of attack. As I was not receiving help from the hospital and insurance bureaucrats, I made my own program for Michael based on my interviews with any and all cancer survivors I could possibly get on the phone.

In the mornings, I'd go to the gym for one hour a day and get pumped up for battle. In retrospect, this was silly because, I mean, cancer is not a boxing opponent, it's a disease. But that didn't stop me from taking it on as if I were the Terminator. If only it were as simple as saying, "Hasta La Vista, Baby."

While I running on the treadmill, I'd listen to inspirational audiobooks. The book of choice at that period was called Relentless: From Good to Great to Unstoppable by Tom S. Grover, a sports coach with a tough attitude. "You will finish your workout at all costs," was his general stance. He talked about how Shaquille O'Neal hires him because he makes Shaquille exercise until he literally throws up. One time, one of the athletes he coached got an injury on his Achilles heel and the author bragged about how under his coaching, the player became so tough that he played through the injury. This book inspired me. "Rah, Rah, Rah, I can beat cancer!" I'd say to myself. "Nothing is stronger than human willpower!"

Back at home, I'd burst through the door with marching-band-level enthusiasm usually reserved for the Macy's Day Parade. I was delusional. Michael could not even lay flat on his back because the fluid in his lungs was so bad that he had trouble breathing. He wasn't sleeping because who can sleep in the upright position on oxygen tanks? It was like trying to sleep in a spacesuit on a Greyhound with seats that don't lean back.

My behavior wasn't comforting, but that wasn't my goal. Winners don't need to be comforted, they need to be pumped up. I made a list of daily tasks on the whiteboard.

Whiteboard Checklist for Healing:

10 glasses of water.

Two shots of injectable CBD oil that I had purchased from the black market.

Three hours of infrared heating treatments on an infrared mattress made from amethyst crystals, which cost a hefty $4400. (I still use it. It's a great product.)

Coriolus Versicolor.

Vitamin C drops.

Epsom salt bath.

Michael could not keep up with the demands of the whiteboard. As it would approach the end of the day, he would only have maybe an eighth of the items on the list completed. I'd admonish him for his lack of commitment.

"You need to stay on it, Michael! Complete the list at all costs!"

"Baby. I can't…I feel nauseous. I can't drink any more water today," Michael would reply weakly.

"Shaquille O'Neal threw up every day as he was training for the NBA, so you drink that water even if you have to throw up all of it!" I am embarrassed to admit I may have picked up some of my tactics from the "Scared Straight" series directed toward troubled teenagers who needed to turn their lives around. "Michael! You need to do this or you are going to die!!"

During this time, his limbs had fluids in them, and I would massage his arms and legs for an hour at a time, to bring down the swelling. He would beg me to stop. "Michael, I know this is uncomfortable, but we need to beat this and we must do our part to keep you alive, Baby," I would tell him.

This went on for a solid month. I was convinced that if we followed this formula, we could save him. We knew that we were not approved for holistic treatment once we went into the emergency room, which would mean a shift from trying to cure him to keeping him comfortable until he died. Western medicine told us there was no hope, while holistic medicine offered us a tiny amount of hope.

I would have done anything to be able to hold on to that as long as possible, but Michael could no longer stand the discomfort. Even with the oxygen tanks turned up at maximum, he still felt as though he was drowning. He could not lay back, we had run out of pills for comfort, and it became clear that neither I nor the home was equipped to take care of him in the way that he needed. It was the most difficult thing in the world to see my partner suffering.

I finally asked Michael what he wanted. "The doctor said that you have about six months to live if we pursue treatment. You are in great pain and I am wondering if it would be easier for you if we made you comfortable. It's okay to take it easy…what do you think?"

He sadly agreed. Before we went to the emergency room, Michael asked to sit with me and spend what would be our last hour together in our home. At first, I responded by breaking down and crying and throwing stuff in the kitchen. Not comforting. But after I calmed down, I sat down in front of him and looked into his sad eyes as he told me how much he loved me. He assured me that he would visit me often from the other side. I told him that in the next lifetime he had to promise not to leave me so soon, as this was so short and unfair.

We held each other and told each other what we appreciated about one another. I told Michael that I give him the credit for most of my funniest stand-up comedy jokes. Michael said, "Thank you for not allowing me to die alone like those washed-up Hollywood actresses," which inspired a tearful chuckle.

"What am I gonna do after you leave me? Half of my jokes are about you," I said, half-joking. "I am going to have to go from a headliner to a feature comedian." (This means going from a 45-minute set to 20 minutes.)

He laughed. "You'll figure it out, Baby. I will always be with you."

During our car ride over to the emergency room, he

asked to take city streets so he could take a last look at his life. I was so blessed to have these final moments with him, as I got to tell him how much he meant to me and he was able to do the same. I am so proud of us that we were able to maintain and express our love for one another until the very last moment.

There is one moment that I will never forget. During one of the trips to the emergency room, Michael woke up in the middle of the night and said, "Where am I?"

In typical Aidan fashion, I yelled in a panic, "Nurse, come quick, it's gone to his brain!"

A nurse ran in. "Sir, who am I? Who am I?" she demanded.

He pointed to her name tag. "You…you are Ethel! You are Lucille Ball's friend!"

The nurse and I could not help but burst into laughter and Michael joined us, although I think he had no idea what we were actually laughing about.

Then Michael pointed to me. "I know that guy, though. Have you met him? That's my boyfriend, Aidan. And Aidan, I am so sorry that you have to spend so much time in the hospital with me. I promise that this year you are gonna get two Christmases and two birthdays, 'cause you deserve it."

In another one of our moments, he thanked me for being his family. He told me he had never understood the value of family as others have talked about it, and now he understood. Michael and I had always been somewhat of loners in this world and I feel the same way about him. I feel he taught me what it means to have a family and love someone unconditionally.

I was so terrified of losing Michael that I had to find hope in a hopeless situation. Without that hope, I would have ended up running around naked in someone's front yard, invoking a magical unicorn to save the day. I thought I could muscle up a solution that we could follow that would force Michael into wellness.

But everyone around me knew that Michael was facing the end and didn't have the heart to tell me. Even Michael knew. It was later revealed that when I was out of the room he told two of our best friends, Cyrus and Tuesday, "He really thinks I'm gonna make it, but can you guys just please make sure that he is happy?"

I hope that by sharing the last days of Michael's life, people will see the value in maintaining hope and optimism. I suppose one could look at this situation and say, "See Aidan? See where all that positivity got you? You still lost Michael." As it turns out, I do not have control over life and death, but I'm so, so grateful to have decided to hold onto hope and optimism, even during these trying times.

Without hope, my last days with Michael would have been even darker. We shared moments of hope and dreamed together of beating cancer and documenting his victory to share with the world. We laughed about how lucky we were to have each other and inspired each other to keep going. Our decision to survive this together demonstrated our commitment to each other and how much love we actually shared.

Losing Michael was difficult and I thought the hard part was over, but I think it was worse after he was gone.

Recollecting and reorganizing the life of someone I loved after they had gone was one of those things it had never occurred to me I'd have to do.

What a nightmare. I loved Michael to tears but he had some design choices for our apartment that were really really difficult to clean up. Like for example, Michael found contact paper, like for cabinets, that he really loved and decided it would look cool to lay them down on the floor over our tiles in the kitchen and living room. The pattern on the contact paper looked like silly strings of different colors just randomly placed together on some kind of digital art application. I never noticed how hideous they were until after Michael died. I guess Michael was so excited about it that I never actually thought about what I thought about it.

I invited my friend Tuesday Thomas over to help me rip up the contact paper. Ripping up contact paper from the floor is hard because it would rip into tiny tiny pieces that Tuesday and I had to be on our knees and pick at each tiny individual piece. We had a good time yelling, "Damn you, Michael, what were you thinking!" as we chipped our fingernails cleaning up his abstract design.

Finding a love letter that he had written to me was tough. He would write me handwritten notes every day for the first few months, then we would just tell each other instead, because one day I ran out of paper.

"Dear Aidan,

I am so grateful to have found you. I love you so much and hope that we can share in our laughter for a very long time together. Also, I can't wait to come home so I can treat you like the filthy, filthy slut that you are. You whore.

Love, Michael

PS. You're my bitch tonight. Also, don't forget to spray the plants down so they don't die."

Michael sure had a way with words.

Then people say things to you that are just oftentimes so unhelpful. I understand. I mean no one knows what to say to a widow who is 33 years old? No one is trained for this! I had two exchanges that stick out in particular. So I present to you now two things never to say to a recent widow:

1) I heard about Michael. I am so sorry. But he was older so...you knew it was coming, right?

He was twenty years older than me, how old did this girl think I was? I said he was older, not geriatric! It's not like he needed my help getting up. I mean. In that way.

2) Don't worry, Aidan, he's with Jesus now.

Great. It made me feel great to know that Michael is sitting on a cloud somewhere hanging out with the most popular guy in the world. Terrific. Of course he left to join Jesus 'cuz why would he want to hang out with me here, when he could be chilling with a guy who literally turns water into wine?!? He's got so many followers and he doesn't even have an Instagram!

I have to say even though people said some things that did not land in the way it was intended, I could see that everyone was doing their best to comfort me. No one was trying to be mean. It's just. Again. What do you say to someone who lost their spouse?

I have to say I was helped during this difficult period by some amazing friends. Nina and Corey were Michael's and my little brother and sister, who often told us that Michael and I were relationship goals. I am sure they meant everything but the dying part. Nina and Corey would call to check in on me often during this difficult time. I had known Nina since she was 14 years old, so I tried to shield her and her boyfriend, attempting to deal with Michael's death without involving them. For months, I didn't even fill Nina in on Michael's cancer, for fear that it would upset her.

But once Nina found out what was happening, she was there for me in a way that showed me she was no longer the teenage girl that I considered to be my lil' sis. She was now a beautiful, intelligent woman who showed me such generosity of spirit. Ironically, the loss of Michael actually brought us closer than ever, as we were both able to be seen for who we really were to each other; she, a grown-up, and me an individual who is vulnerable at times.

Jana, a beautiful friend and spirit, also one of the toughest and hardworking women ever to walk the earth, invited me to spend an entire month with her to forget my troubles and do a contract job with her for a political campaign. She never left my side. I cried so much during that month and I kept wanting to listen to sad songs. "Graduation" by Vitamin C was the song that would make me cry all the time.

As we go on,

We remember,

All the times we,

Had together,

And as our lives change,

Come whatever,

We will still be,

Friends forever.

"Come whatever. Friends forever." What a brilliant rhyme. It made me cry. I imagine this is how sophomores feel when their boyfriends are seniors and they go off to college while the sophomores are still stuck at PS 118. Jana would let me listen to the song on loop multiple times a day and never tried to "make it all okay." She let me be wherever I was during that month and I am forever grateful for her generosity and thoughtfulness.

Leah went to pick up the ashes with me in the basement of the USC Hospital. Michael and I had decided that if he passed away to let the hospital handle the cremation for me to pick up so I wouldn't have to deal with the transporting of the body. We kept riding the elevator up and down because it literally looked like a furnace area that you might find in "Nightmare on Elm Street." So crazy. There was no door that was marked "Mortuary" or anything. Finally we stopped a doctor who looked terrified to speak to us as he pointed to an unmarked door through which sat two Latina ladies who asked us to sign out for Michael's ashes. They offered Leah and me bite-sized Snickers.

I remember walking through the parking lot, carrying Michael. I started to freak out because holding him in a box in my hands felt like too much for me. I said to Leah, "I don't know if I can keep him in my house until I have to spread him." Leah generously offered to keep him until I spread him and I almost handed Michael over, then I stopped myself. NO. I would not abandon Michael now. I would see this through all the way to the end and not hand him off for someone else. Leah gave me a huge hug and told me she was proud of me. Just hearing those words that someone thought positively of how I was handling it meant so much. I felt infinitely alone since Michael had gone and Leah, for a moment, made me feel close to someone.

Then it was time to spread the ashes. Michael had this weird obsession with creeks and rivers and he actually asked that his ashes be spread in the Sierra mountains in Central California. My friends Tuesday and Cyrus joined me on this journey. I love those guys. We started comedy together! Cyrus and I did our very first comedy show together, and Tuesday and I met in a basement where an open mic was being held. Cyrus, Tuesday, and I used to run a weekly show together at the Clown House, which is a storefront comedy spot on Skid Row in Downtown Los Angeles, where they have over 600 clown figurines crammed into a 300 square-foot area.

Cyrus, Tuesday, Michael, and I were very close because Tuesday and Cyrus ran the Friday night variety show called Freakshow which has grown into a massive and successful brand of shows that tours all over the country, while Michael helped me run the show on Saturdays which was just a plain ol' comedy show called Clownhouse Comedy. Not as creative as "Freakshow," which is probably why it's no longer running. The four of us would hang out, week after week. We ran shows together, helped each other with jokes (which Michael was always excited to chime in on), and griped about the trials and tribulations of being a new comic in Los Angeles.

When you are a new comic, you get treated badly

sometimes, and Cyrus, Tuesday, and I were no exceptions to the rule. While the three of us discussed what was happening in the comedy world, Michael was always there. We loved having Michael as someone who was a neutral non-comedian party who would listen and offer his opinion. Michael was the kind of person that once he decided you were his friend, you could do no wrong. Whatever we griped about, Michael just sat there in his New York fashion and said, "Screw that guy he's an asshole," or "Who needs them?" any time any one of us felt we were being messed with.

Tuesday and Cyrus kept up the tradition of ribbing and razzing on the day we were driving up together to spread the ashes. Tuesday got in the car, looked at Michael's urn and said, "Wow, Michael. You need some lotion? You are looking ashy today." Which made us all bust out into hysterics.

Cyrus chimed in. "Yeah man...you look like you've lost a lot of weight."

I know Michael well enough to know that this was the kind of send-off he would have wanted. He hated melodramatics and whining. Even in my writing this book I can almost hear him say, "Okay, Aidan, enough of the sappy stuff. Finish the chapter -- Lets go! Lets go!!"

On the way up to spread his ashes, we listened to Michael's favorite disco hits. Lime, an Italian hippie married couple who looked like they were in their 40's, and whose male member later came out as trans. Fun Fun, another Italian duo where they just got two pretty girls who lip synced while jumping around in bounce houses (not kidding). And of course, Sheryl Lee Ralph, who if you don't know, played Moesha's mom in Brandy's '90s sitcom. Did you know Sheryl had a hit called "In the Evening" from 1985? I didn't. But it was Michael's favorite song. It's about someone who works and lives like a normal person during the day, but in the evening, comes to life.

"These '80s gay anthems are so funny," Cyrus said. "They are always about coming out at night. Like, they are all straight bank tellers by day, but in the evening, watch out for the taffeta!"

I have really cool friends.

Even with the good friends that I had helping me through it was still an impossible time for me, emotionally. I would regularly just sit and text his phone number that I kept on for 3 months past his death just so I could feel connected to him. I hoped that somehow, he would see the texts I was sending him. "I love you, you know that right?" No response. Ugh. I deleted his name from my phone but I knew his number by heart.

I reached a breaking point when I started researching options for suicide. It was scary how serious I was about committing suicide. I went shopping online for guns. I was trying to find discount codes for handguns until I realized what I was doing. *I'm bargain-hunting for my suicide weapon! How cheap does one have to be to be bargain hunting for a suicide weapon? How stupid is that? I mean if there was ever a time to put something on a credit card, wasn't this it? I guess I just didn't want to get a bad deal. After all I may be suicidal but I am a smart shopper right? I mean I don't want people to get one over on me and think I was born yesterday! I mean… I'll be dead tomorrow but…*

Then I thought, *well, if I kill myself who is going to clean up the mess?* (I'm a people pleaser, through and through.) So I thought I would buy a helium tank and suffocate myself but then I thought, what if I succeed and then my spirit is caught inside the helium tank?!

I told my mom I wanted to kill myself and she said, "I stayed alive for you when I was suicidal after your grandmother passed away -- so stay strong."

"Well, Mother, then maybe we should both kill ourselves, since we are only staying alive to support one another. If we both kill ourselves then we don't have to be here in this miserable place any longer only because of each other." That was a new low. I was not only contemplating my own suicide but I essentially told my mother to kill herself. I think my mother knew how serious I was in my suicidal thoughts, and it scared the crap out of her. I still regret this conversation.

Thank God for Judge Judy because, honestly, the reason I didn't kill myself was because of one particular episode. There was an Asian woman around my mother's age having to deal with paperwork and she was getting reamed for her lack of preparation. I thought, "If I kill myself, my mom has to go through court and stuff. She would have to deal with this kind of stuff and that would really suck and what if the judge yells at her? I can't do that to her." Okay keep in mind I was kind of wonky during this time and not thinking clearly but, hey. Whatever it takes to keep a girl alive, am I right?

So I resolved to stay on Earth. But I made a deal with myself...."Okay, I will stay on Earth but if I have to stay, I don't want to feel this miserable. I refuse to feel this bad.

This sucks sucks sucks sucks sucks." My editor told me that I should just say sucks one time but I really want to make the point so -- SUCKS SUCKS SUCKS SUCKS SUCKS!!!

I had never ever experienced such extreme levels of negative feelings before in my life. The level of pain I was in was such that I feel if I did actually kill myself...who could have blamed me? I mean, real talk, I didn't have kids or responsibilities so it might have been understood by the community. I'm 34. If I were gonna die at 94 (since Asians live forever), I figured, wow, 60 years is a long, long time to be miserable. Each minute feels like an hour when you are in an emotional tone of misery! That's 3600 years. I. DON'T. WANT. TO. LIVE. THAT. LONG!

My friends told me "give it time" and I remember saying to them, "No! This misery is something that I cannot live with for another second. I can't. It hurts too much, and I refuse. Besides, I need something to keep me occupied and giving it time is just waiting, which blows. That BLOWS!"

I made a decision to figure out how to find happiness again. I committed myself. I would figure out how to stay here and find joy. I would apply everything I had learned in my life up until this point to try to give myself joy again. This was a departure from past experiences because in my life up to this point, my goal-setting had always been about the accomplishment of things but this time it was different. My goal was positive emotion. I had to give myself hope for something better. So I forged ahead to the great unknown.

Grief and loss is a painful reality of life.

If you are struggling, flash the QR code below for a message from Aidan.

CHAPTER 5

A Tactical Approach to Happiness

I approached happiness with a science student's mindset and attempted to break down what happy really meant. I noticed that people threw around the word "happy," a lot! Are you happy? Yes, I'm happy! Shery Crow said, "If it makes you happy, it can't be that bad." Pharrell said he was, "Happy." Then I turned my attention to what I always turn my attention to when I want to learn something. Reality television. Namely, a show called "Dance Moms."

"Dance Moms" is a show about the Abby Lee Dance Company, based out of Pittsburgh. Abby Lee Dance Company is run by the head dance teacher Abby Lee who is this woman who I've never seen actually dance. She looks nothing like a dancer. I mean, no shade, but she is at least 250 pounds and can't stand for too long. Then she gathers all of her dancers up and conducts the pyramid which is her way of ranking the dancers based on how well they did for the team in the prior week.

If you are on the bottom of the pyramid, she berates you. "On the bottom of the pyramid -- (dramatic reveal and music) -- is Paige. Paige, you messed up the dance combination and you looked lost out there. Get it together! Where was your head? You keep screwing up! Remember everyone is replaceable, and I won't have a loser on my team!" Paige is like, seven years old.

After Abby gets done berating all of the girls on the team and making them feel like they have no worth outside of the quality of their fan kicks, she assigns the solo dances and parts in the group dance. This is where the dance moms come in.

Moms start yelling stuff like:

"Why is Brooke in the back again after she was on the top of the pyramid?"

or

"Chloe is a way better dancer than Nia and should have gotten the solo!"

or

"Can you please stop throwing chairs at my daughter!"

Which Abby gets a wind of and starts yelling back things like:

"All you moms need to shut up!"

or

"I wouldn't have thrown the chair if your daughter could do a proper layout!"

All of this happens in front of the young girls, by the way. If you have never seen the show, I would not suggest it because almost everyone I recommend it to says, "What is wrong with you? I don't understand the appeal of this." But I think everyone secretly watches, because Michael loved "Dance Moms." He was ashamed of it, but he loved it. I know, because every time it would come on, he would pretend to be doing something else, and yet he knew everything that was happening on the show.

On one episode, one dance mom yelled at another, "YOU ARE A HORRIBLE MOTHER AND NOTHING BUT A LAZY-EYED LOSER WITH A KID WHO CAN'T DANCE!"

Michael yelled out from the kitchen, "Baby! Was that Yolanda?!?" Eventually, Michael admitted he loved "Dance Moms," although he claimed that it wasn't the same for him since JoJo left.

During the months after Michael's passing, I ate a lot of sweets and watched a lot of "Dance Moms." I was researching happiness. There were only a handful of happy moments in seven seasons of Dance Moms, but I noted it every time someone on the show said that they were happy.

"I am happy that I got on the cheerleading squad."

"I am happy we won."

"I am happy to have had such a romantic night with my husband."

"I am happy that I don't have a face that looks like yours."

"I am happy!" (This last one was slurred during a trip to New Orleans where the moms went day drinking. It ended in a fist-fight on the street and lawsuits between the mothers.)

I noticed that the dance moms were happy based

on what was happening around them. If circumstances were good, YAY! If circumstances were bad, boo! So I thought, *okay I will just create as many YAY experiences in my life as possible.* I took a tactical approach to happiness.

TACTIC 1: **Go on Dates.**

This was a terrible plan, any way you slice it. I get it. 100%. But at the time, I felt like this was a good idea. I could keep busy and eat free, hot meals with hot guys, and have hot sex! Seemed like a good idea to me!

It turns out, I was not ready to date, whatsoever. I would show up and leak trauma all over my dates. A typical conversation sounded like this:

Date: Hi! My name is Jeff.

Aidan: Hi! I'm Aidan, nice to meet you. How was your day, but first, could you tell me if you have any history of cancer in your immediate family?

Or:

Date: I love what I do. I am an engineer for Microsoft.

Aidan: That's nice -- are you currently on any medication for diabetes or any other chronic health conditions? Can your doctor fax me the results of your most recent physical?

These were less like dates and more like health questionnaires. Naturally, this did not yield good results. But I was so deep in my trauma I did not know why I was failing at connecting with my dates, and this affected my self-esteem.

My brilliant solution was to lead with sex, so they could find out what a good lay I am and that would keep them coming back for more. This tactic did yield better results because -- I am damn good -- but the downside was that men could get what they wanted sexually without having to take me seriously. After they were done, men could not get away from me fast enough.

I believe there is something to the "vibrational tone" theory which suggests that people respond to your vibes and not what you say or do. I was giving off vibes of, "I'm broken -- help me!," which attracted people who fed on my vulnerabilities. I did not know such people existed in the world but, boy, did I find out.

One particularly traumatic experience came from a friend of mine who had been supportive through Michael's death. Let's call this friend, "Paul." Paul was a healthcare professional and was a mutual friend of myself and Michael. During Michael's illness, Paul suggested many helpful things. He told us what pills Michael should take, what kinds of healthy foods to buy, and suggested the Vitamin C IV drip treatment that eased Michael's pain in his last days. I am grateful to Paul for all of this... HOWEVER...

Paul and I had lunch a couple of months after Michael's death and, feeling that I could trust him, I laid everything on the table. I told him about my vulnerabilities and how I felt suicidal. I told him about my resolve to be happy and how I thought that going on dates was a good way to distract myself. I told him about how poorly all of that was going. Paul suggested that instead of dating random men that I didn't know, I should be around people that I knew.

In the weeks after, Paul texted me every day and sent me photos of wherever he was. He was a perfect gentleman.

No dick pics to be found! He asked me about my emotional well-being and we had long conversations. We started flirting and he eventually invited me over one night to spend time with him. Ugh...I was such an idiot. I was not physically attracted to him but was very attracted to the type of person he presented himself to be.

I went over there and he made me a nice dinner. Then we started having sex. He said something like, "I understand what pain you might be in, so any time you feel uncomfortable, please let me know."

Then he suggested that we should go to a gay bathhouse (a sex club) because it would be fun to have sex in front of people there!

Confused, but wanting not to disappoint, I said, "Sure."

We got there and after a few hours, he decided that we should go over to his friend's house where he was conducting an orgy. By the way, I had no car. Paul was my ride. So we headed over to the orgy and there was a couple there. Paul and I switched partners and my new partner immediately fell asleep.

I tried to be understanding because these kinds of things happen. So, politely, I sat in the room while Paul had sex with his (awake) partner and I played Candy Crush on my phone. After (I am not kidding) 90 minutes, I tried to get in on the action. Paul brushed me off and told me to wait until he was done with his friend. So I waited another 30 minutes before asking if we could leave.

"What, are you gonna get all needy on me now, Aidan?" Paul demanded.

Shocked and confused, I just sat back. Pretty soon after, he was done and we were on our way back to his place. In the car, Paul said, "You were acting pretty needy there, Aidan. It's very unattractive. You should work on that."

When we finally got to his place, he told me to take my shirt off. Then he pointed to my chest and laughed. "You have boobs like a girl."

I just didn't know what to say. He had been so nice but all of the sudden, it was like Dr. Jekyll/Mr. Hyde. Then he asked me to sit down on his couch and said, "You wanna see something?" He pulled out a handgun from his dresser drawer. "What do you think?"

My first thought was to say, "I think it's convenient," grab the gun, and shoot him dead right then and there. I think his intent was to inspire fear in me, but what it did was make me want to punch his lights out. He was the one who should have been scared. Nothing is scarier than a person who has nothing to live for and nothing to lose.

Now, I take responsibility for my terrible choices. I should not have tried to date or whatever after losing Michael so quickly. At the time, I just thought it would bring me happiness. But, wow. I had never ever been insulted by anyone the way I was by Paul that night, and I attribute this to the fact that I was so vulnerable. Predatory people are good at sniffing out vulnerable candidates.

A few weeks later, I met a man named… lets call him Mel. Mel was very successful man with a very kind heart, but had a huge problem with not knowing what he wanted. Mel was a self-proclaimed bi-sexual man who had never come out of the closet to anyone as having ever dated or having had interest in a man. It was appropriate I met Mel when I did because he was just getting out of a 20-year marriage to a woman with whom he had two kids. Mel got divorced around the same time I lost Michael, so we had similar wounds of having lost the sense of familiarity and routine that we'd had in our daily lives.

At the core, I believe that Mel is a very kind person and I wish him the best in the world. I learned a lot from him. I was a hardworking, top-of-his-field consultant, he generously shared his business acumen. He taught me how to ask for what I deserved and to value what I had to offer. He even helped me increase my self-esteem by encouraging me to present myself in the best way possible.

He let me talk about Michael and cried with me when I shared my memories. I could tell Mel sincerely cared for me, in his own way. However, Mel and I were each in a state of confusion. Me, not knowing how to pick up the pieces after the Michael died, and Mel having to face his desire to date men. Mel was not even out of the closet yet to anyone, other than his wife -- and only then because she had caught him with another man, which eventually and understandably led to the dissolution of his relationship with her.

Both of us were lonely and scared and were intensely physically attracted to each other. I could tell that deep in his heart, Mel wanted to be self-expressed but having hid his own sexuality for so long, he did not know how to do that. He still felt that he had to hide who he really was in order to get what he wanted.

This was a big part of what did our relationship in. Mel would often tell me half-truths and omit key pieces of information in his communication to me, which I would feel hurt to discover later. It started from the very beginning, when he told me he was 38 but was actually 52. He's a great looking 52! He's also a terrible-looking 38. I just assumed he had worked out in the sun for many years. Maybe he had worked on a ranch! Maybe he was a tanning enthusiast! Also, on his dating profile, he boasted an eight-inch you-know-what and that he loved Asian guys. How stupid is it to lie to Asians of all people about measurements? I will just leave that there.

Mel also could not fully express what he wanted. He shared fantasies about three-ways and group sex, however, once he realized I was monogamous, he would try to pretend like he wanted to pursue monogamy. But then, any time he'd had a few drinks, he would eye fuck other attractive men, right in front of me. He could not help it. The compulsion was too strong for him to manage. This led to a lot of embarrassing moments when I would bring him to watch me perform at comedy clubs and people could catch him leering.

Also, I was a secret to the people in his world, which added to the growing distrust that I felt. A lot of my friends like to tell me that they thought he was cheating on me and was just going after what he wanted. Honestly, I prefer to hold the belief that he was a lost soul who was trying to make his way through life. I will never know 100% if he was faithful to me or not, and since I will never know, I am going to choose to believe that his intentions were good.

Not to blame the whole thing on Mel, certainly. I was nowhere near ready for a relationship, given where I was emotionally, and I have major trust issues anyway. I mean my husband died, so I guess it's understandable. but I've always had trust issues. My dad had a whole other family! I grew up with the woman who led her whole life protecting herself against that same injury. So again, understandable, but it doesn't dismiss the fact that it adds a level of difficulty to dating me.

Mel and I pushed each other's most sensitive buttons. Mel had a hard time with being seen as untrustworthy. At the same time, my mistrust grew and grew each time I found yet another piece of information he had not communicated honestly -- or when I'd catch him doing something that he said he would not do (such as texting other potential hookups while I was over at his place). Eventually, I was unable to tell the difference between where my trust issues ended and Mel's half-truths began.

I became more and more distrustful until everything Mel did triggered me. He looked at men and I would get suspicious. He looked at women and I would get suspicious. I got so suspicious that I actually sat down and wrote out the mathematical equation for the likelihood of my getting cheated on if I were with a gay man versus if I were with a bi-sexual man.

Gay Man:

Take 100% of the population:

Women are out, roughly 50% remain in the dating pool.

The man also must be gay. Roughly 10% of the population is gay, so 5% remain for me.

Guys I date really tend to like Asians. Asians in the US 2%. 2% of 5% is .1% of the population.

If I have an attractiveness rating of 30%, which means 30% of the population I like, likes me back.

30% of .1% is .03% of the population.

The solution is that .03 % is the percentage of the population that holds the potential to be my boyfriend.

Bi Man:

100% of the population (we are leaving .03% to add back in later from the male end).

Adding in the other 50 but we are deleting the 10% of GAY WOMEN, and leaving the 90% of STRAIGHT WOMEN. 45% of the population.

2% Asian of 45% is .9%

30% attractive rating is roughly .3%

So, the bi man has .33% available to him while gay guy has only .03%. That's 11 times the number of people he has available to cheat on me with.

I stand by my math but eventually realized that bisexuality was not the problem. It was my mistrust of Mel that was the real culprit. Mel led me to believe that it was my insecurity and hurt that caused my suspicions of him. He acted as though he was the good guy for being understanding, which I now recognize as total bunk. Mel displayed a lack of integrity with a habit of secrecy and what I think is a questionable moral center.

After all, if he had cheated on his wife why would he not cheat on me? Was I correct in this assessment? I am unsure. Do I have a right to try to assess his behavior with me based on his past? I am unsure about that also. All I know is that there were enough factors at play that caused me to mistrust the fellow. I could be wrong about all of it. I also don't care to find out.

I learned a very valuable lesson from my experience with Mel, however. Whether you are right or wrong, if your significant other weakens your ability to trust yourself, he is not the one for you. Clarity and surety are keys to empowerment and we must strengthen those tools if we are to be effective in whatever we choose to pursue. Again, it comes back to deciding whether something is life-giving or death-dealing.

I wish good luck to Mel. I am sure he will be great for someone but he and I were not a match. I thank him for many moments of genuine happiness. That said, the Mel thing broke my heart. Michael was like the AIDS virus in my system and Mel was the cold that did me in. After Mel, I continued to fly even deeper off the handle. Which lead me to my second tactic.

TACTIC 2: *Just forget about it all and HAVE FUN!*

So, Mel and I were supposed to go to Italy together for Thanksgiving. I had my plane ticket, places to stay all set up, and we were going to be on our way. Then I learned another one of Mel's cover-ups, at which point I said, "Screw Italy. I'll get there on my own," and cancelled my trip.

My friends all thought I was an idiot. "Take the trip, Stupid!" is what they all said, but I was not about to spend 10 days in a foreign country with a man I didn't trust. Nope. I watched enough Dateline NBC to know that wasn't a good idea. So I chose to stay home.

This was my first Thanksgiving after Michael's death and I had left 10 days completely empty on my calendar in anticipation for my trip to Italy. I found myself on Thanksgiving Day, the day in which I was supposed to be on the plane to a trip of a lifetime, alone in my apartment with no plans. I thought to myself. *Screw it all. I am going to have fun if it kills me.* I packed my bags and went off -- destination unknown.

I ended up in Modesto, California. I did not know where I was going, I just drove and drove until I ended up there. At the Clarion Inn off of Highway 99. In Modesto, there is a junior college, a Walmart, a Target with a Starbucks in it, and -- that is all.

So I went down to the Walmart, which was the only store that was open, and picked myself up a rotisserie chicken. I took it back to my hotel room, sat on the bed, and turned the TV on to a Real Housewives marathon. I didn't even like the housewives. I never found them entertaining but for some reason rich women squabbling brought me a strange sense of comfort in that dusty motel in Modesto.

After I polished off the chicken, I decided to go on Grindr and check out the men in the area. I'm cute, so a guy offered to come over right away for a hook-up, and, like an Uber-Eats delivery, boom! He was at my door in 15 minutes. I mean, Modesto is small, but this was a five-star, lightning-fast delivery.

This gentleman dressed like Eminem from the 1990s. I imagined that before he'd come over, he'd been chilling in front of a 7-11 with a backwards cap and a bottle of beer wrapped in a brown paper bag. I thought, *WOW. HOT.*

He entered and we shook hands. Yeah. We shook hands. As if he'd just walked into a bank and I was going to help him open a new account. He sat and we made small talk.

"Do you like Modesto?" I asked.

"It sucks...."

Silence.

Okay....Then he pulled out paraphernalia. Drugs. Now, I am no angel and I have dabbled with drugs from time to time, but I got the impression that I was about to get into the major leagues with this one. This dude had a whole spread of contraptions; different lighters of different strengths, a straw for snorting, even a needle and rubber for injections. Holy Crap. The only time I had done anything was orally or snorting through a rolled up dollar bill. This guy brought an actual straw!

I did all of the drugs with him. I didn't do the needles cuz I was too scared but I figured, *What the hell, it's Thanksgiving! Time to party and have fun with this guy I don't know! YAY!*

Not yay.

I am an extremely high-energy individual. So high-energy in fact, that drugs don't actually work on me. I feel good for like an hour and then I end up in the land of Paranoia. It happens so fast. It's like the cells in my body are like, *Dude. You are already extra. We quit. You are on your own.* Within one hour I was looking out the window saying, "They are watching us!" My new friend reminded me we were on the third floor. I was not comforted. "People can scale windows!" I said. That freaked him and he was out of there. He took all of his contraptions with him.

Feeling dejected and lonely, I went back on Grindr and found another guy. Literally his opening hello was, "Do you wanna F***."

"Yeh come over."

He didn't have a car or enough money for an Uber and so I called an Uber for him to be picked up and brought over. My apologies to Clarion Hotel. Anyhow, he came over, and he also had drugs. Funny, I didn't even ask him if he did drugs but I guess people in Modesto just do drugs?

This guy and I...oh my God. The chemistry was amazing. I mean I am still not sure if it was real or fake cause we were both high, but we were at it for like seven or eight hours. Then we fell asleep and cuddled all night! For a minute there, I thought I had found love again.

We woke up in the morning, and there I was thinking we might chill and get some breakfast. But he informed me that he had to go home and get ready to meet his girlfriend. What?!? I mean, I knew that our chances of making it were slim because, you know, he is a drug addict that lives 300 miles away -- but, girlfriend? Then I find out that he is on the DL and also now he is in a shame spiral.

"Can I get an Uber back to my house? I should have money -- I am such a fuck-up."

I attempted to make small talk. "Were you always in Modesto?"

"No, I've made mistakes in my life."

Wow. He could not get away from me fast enough. He jetted. I was alone again. So I drove myself back home and went to sleep.

KIDDING. I got back to LA and went on Grindr again and looked for another guy. This time, I was actively looking for a man to do drugs with so I could forget about all my troubles. I went to another guy's house and he offered me GHB. This is the stuff that Cosby used to make his victims pass out. I took this drug. Voluntarily. At this guys house. I passed out cold in the middle of fooling around. Ugh.

He woke me up and told me to leave. He was upset that I fell asleep. The only problem was that I couldn't stand up straight. The room was spinning and I couldn't make it to the door. He threatened to call the police if I didn't leave immediately. I asked for a glass of water.

"I will give you water on the way out," he said. "Now, get the hell out. You are a loser."

I stumbled out the door and somehow made my way back into my car where my head was spinning so hard that I couldn't do anything but lay there and think about what I had done. John/Jeff/Steve (I don't remember his name) was right. I was a loser.

Even before Michael died, I had had tons of training in self-development, I had been a life coach for people, I had been a speaker advocating for LGBT rights. I had a brand on Instagram as the person who gives people good advice. Kids in Tennessee would email me asking me what to do about coming out as gay. My friends and colleagues looked to me to strengthen the voice of the LGBT comedy community. I was not supposed to be like this. A drug-addicted loser. I felt like such a fraud.

I missed Michael. I started to get angry because I felt if he hadn't died on me I wouldn't be like this. I was angry with Mel for lying to me. Pissed at the Modesto Uber guy for being on the DL. Strangely, I totally understood why that guy's name I don't remember would kick me out. I was kind of glad he did instead of calling an ambulance. That would've been way worse.

(I will put a note in here that everyone on my team who has read this part of the book is really really angry at Steve?/Sean?/James?/Pat?/Tartuffe? And that I should be more outraged. Honestly I am angrier at Mel because I cared about that guy. GHB Guy cared about me as much I cared about him -- and that was -- not much.)

In true Aidan fashion, I rallied my strength. *NO. I will not blame everyone else! I will take responsibility for my own life and get myself together! I am strong! I am powerful! I am not a loser! I am going to work hard and prove to myself that I am worthy!* So I decided to try my next tactic to find happiness.

TACTIC 3: *Good Behavior*

Drugs and men didn't work out for me, so I decided that if I put myself fully into productive things, I would become much happier. So, in the month after I had made this decision, I did the following:

Started going to gym class every day, sometimes twice a day.

Cut all carbs from my diet.

Got a job writing articles for a newspaper.

Took on a promotion with my bubble business as scheduler and manager in addition to trainer.

Created content for online websites freelance.

Wrote at least one hour every day.

Booked at least two comedy shows every night.

Started producing four comedy shows a month (up from two).

Booked myself road gigs for comedy where I would have to travel every weekend.

Took on a political consulting job as a contract in rural Washington.

Does that sound impossible? Well, I did it. All of it. I was driven by my need to prove my worth and make damn sure that I was an upstanding member of society. I was not going to be a statistic. I was not going to be a loser. I was not going to be a hypocrite. Rah, Rah, Rah. Work. Work. Work. Tired? Take an Adderall and work more. Still Tired? Pot of coffee.

Between my anxiety, depression, and workload, I was averaging around four hours of sleep a night. I had my first panic attack in Colorado, luckily around friends, so it wasn't a big deal. Actually, it's a huge deal because people just don't have panic attacks every day. That's like saying, "I just had a mental breakdown and was 5150'd, but no worries. It's part of being a teen star." Emergency room visits due to panic attacks are not normal. But nonetheless, I survived it. Rah. Rah. So, what did I do as soon as I got out? That same evening, I went to a gym class.

It was panic attack number two that really created a problem for me. I took a contract job working in Washington state, trying to get people to sign propositions for tougher gun laws. I probably worked 12 hours a day doing this. I had no idea that people felt so strongly about gun laws. I was told to, "Go back to China," more times in Olympia, Washington, than I would like to count. Things were not much better in Tacoma, Washington. Don't mess with guns.

One day, I was driving through rural Washington and I started to feel my heart flutter. Very, very quickly. I noticed that I could not breathe and so I pulled over and drank some water, which caused me to have severe nausea. Then I puked up the water, and I became convinced that I had eaten something raw. So I sat on the side of the road, trying to throw up. For three hours.

EMTs and a police car showed up to see if everything was okay. I said I just had food poisoning but in reality I had no idea what was happening. They asked me a few questions and then they asked me politely to make my way over to the gas station so I could be safely off the road.

I made myself drive to a rural gas station, where I spent another two hours heaving, as nothing was coming up. As I was gagging, a man walked up and all I could see was his feet.

"Can I pray for you?" he asked.

I said, "Sure." I thought he meant, 'thoughts and prayers', like on Facebook. Like digital prayers. You know, the kind that just sends positive vibes and then people can get likes on it. Nope. He meant the real thing.

He put his hand on my back, raised his other hand to the sky, and full-on started screaming. "LORD, PLEASE HELP THIS MAN FEEL BETTER! PLEASE LORD!"

I had to stop heaving for a moment. What exactly was happening? I looked up. I am not kidding when I say he looked just like the guy from Nickelback. You know those long, curly, blonde locks? Also, he was wearing an affinity t-shirt. With sequins sewn onto it.

A crowd was starting to gather. They are all white in Washington state. So I looked up at Nickelback Guy, looked at the concerned white faces hovering over me. Past them, I could see grass. And cows. *Moo.* All I could think was, *wow, this is what purgatory must feel like.*

I prayed with him. I mean, why not? What had I got to lose at this point? Screw it. After about five minutes that felt like five hours, he wished me, "good luck," and then left. Strange, he never asked me if I needed water or food or anything of the sort. He just prayed and walked away.

I thought maybe if I put some food in my system, I would feel better, so I walked into the gas station where I suddenly felt my body freeze up completely. I could not feel my fingers or hands and I saw that I was making fists but I could not release them. I fell to the floor and asked someone to call an ambulance.

As I sat on the floor, crying, all I could say through my tears was, "I am so, so sorry I am interrupting your business. I will buy a full tank of gas after this, I promise." Of course, I thought I was going to die, so I was lying to them.

The ambulance arrived. It was the same EMT that asked me to move off the road a few hours earlier. I dissolved into tears. "I am so sorry for interrupting this business and I am so sorry for wasting tax dollars." The EMT gave me a hug. I couldn't believe it. She was so nice.

I thought I was going to be dead for real. Definitely having a heart attack. To be honest, I was happy about it. I thought, *Well, I didn't commit suicide and I tried my best and I will at least get to see Michael again. I am coming, Mike!* Nope. Just a panic attack. Nothing wrong with my heart. My first thought was, *Dammit.*

After I was stabilized, I went back into the gas station and offered to buy a bunch of things and the clerk said, "Please don't worry about it. Take good care of yourself, Sweetness," which made me cry again. When you feel so isolated and so alone, any bit of kind words helps.

So. My "tactics" were not going to work. I only featured three in this chapter, but I didn't mention trying to go out every night with friends, or binge watching TV, or binge eating, pedicures, manicures, facials. Nothing I was doing was working to make me happier. I got the distinct feeling that my approach to the whole happiness thing was off. Tactics to focused on achievements, environment, and circumstances were not going to bring me happiness.

You know how millionaires always say money doesn't bring you happiness? Well, I knew this to be true. I know so many miserable millionaires. I also know people who thought that they would be happy once they were in a relationship, then they revert back to their old level of happiness once they get into one. Ditto for people with job promotions. So then how could I raise my level of happiness?

As Aidan learned the hard way...
Happinness is difficult to improve by mere fixing
of your life situations.

For more on this topic, flash the QR code below.

CHAPTER 6

The Emotion Principle

I met with my friend Jackie for lunch soon after the gas station incident. I broke down into tears as I described the experience.

The topic of the day was: Missing Michael. Again. It had only been maybe five months and I was in a worse emotional state than I had ever been in and on the verge of another complete meltdown. I started thinking, *wouldn't it be funny if I had another panic attack right now and the ambulance showed up and it was the same girl from Washington State? Maybe she would give me another hug and she could take a piece of this calamari.*

Jackie said something that I had never ever heard before, "Whenever you feel bad, sad, lonely, or longing for him -- try to figure out the specific emotion that you think you are missing from not having Michael, and then try to provide that for yourself."

I contemplated for a moment and then thought, *what kind of crystal-holding, woo-woo, mumbo-jumbo is this girl trying to sell me?*

"Where did you hear this?" I asked.

"YouTube," Jackie said.

I stared at her blankly.

"There is this woman named Esther on YouTube who channels a being named Abraham. Abraham comes through Esther to deliver messages from the universe."

I blinked. I thought to myself, *I am getting tips for life from Jackie, who is getting messages from Esther, a psychic channeler on YouTube, who is receiving messages from Abraham, who is delivering messages from the universe. What has my life become? This has got to be the most convoluted game of telephone I have ever heard.*

"How did you find Esther?" I asked.

"I think I'm an alien, so I looked for proof of life on other planets and Abraham confirmed there was."

I love my friends. I have the most incredible, caring, wonderful, and eccentric friends in the world. No matter how kooky they may seem on the outside, they all have hearts of gold, and I am so appreciative of them. Even my alien friends have hearts of gold. Thanks, Jackie.

So, Jackie sent me a video by "Abraham Hicks" and one articulated this principle: "There is no desire that anyone holds for any other reason than that they believe they will feel better in the achievement of it. Whether it is a material object, a physical state of being, a relationship, a condition, or a circumstance - at the heart of every desire is the desire to feel good. And so, the standard of success in life is not the things or the money - the standard of success is absolutely the amount of joy you feel."

I thought this was an interesting concept. So I looked back to what I had been trying to achieve with my tactics. In pursuing a relationship with Mel, what could I have been going for? What possible feelings could he have provided for me? I went home and made a list.

Why I wanted to Date Mel:

He was nice.

He believed in me.

He was supportive through my heartaches.

I looked at the list and thought, *okay, this is nice, but the reasons listed above were not emotional. If Mel is nice, what emotional payoff would I get by having a boyfriend who was nice? I would feel supported. Supported. Safety. Safety!* Not completely, of course, but a part of the reason why I wanted to date Mel was because of the emotional payoff of SAFETY.

This made a ton of sense to me. I felt clinical and kind of cold to breakdown a relationship in this way but it rang very true that when I was with Mel and we were having a good day together, I felt a great sense of safety! More so than I would have felt if I were alone. Therefore, I was using my relationship to give myself a greater sense of safety. Mel = safety. "…At the heart of every desire is the desire to feel good…" *Huh. Very interesting.* I moved on to the next item on the list of the emotional payoffs that Mel provided for me.

"Mel believed in me." What emotional payoff did I get by dating someone who "believed in me?" Support! And also, courage. Courage to know that I was on the right track. By having someone on my side who "believed in me," I felt talented and worthy, which brought to me a sense of courage to command more money when doing comedy shows or negotiating contracts. Mel helped me feel more valuable as an individual in the area of my talent and abilities.

"Mel made me feel supported through my heartaches." I felt heard. Safety. Again. Understood. Okay, understood is not really a feeling. No still not really a feeling right? Calm. Open. Worthy. Sane. Valid. Whoa. Okay.

This concept completely blew my mind so I started using this technique with every other thing that I thought I wanted. So I went to the next item that I tried to get. Sex with strangers on drugs -- why did I want that? My first instinct was to say, "Because you are a loser, Aidan," but thank God I am good at keeping on topic. I told myself, "Yes, I might be a loser, but that's not the exercise at hand, Dorkus. What was the emotional payoff?" So I made another list.

Sex with Strangers on Drugs:

Suppression of overwhelming anxiety.

Excitement.

Reminder of what I used to have with Michael.

Wow, this was deep. In the Thanksgiving craziness, I actually had used the drugs as a way to calm myself and forget my troubles. I was in a lot of pain and I just wanted to stop feeling the pain. So I went straight for the drugs, which created a synthetically positive feeling when I couldn't generate it naturally. I just wanted to feel better.

This realization actually calmed me down a good

deal and allowed me to have some empathy for myself. I had been so busy calling myself a loser for everything that I hadn't actually taken the time to acknowledge what a difficult year I had had. I lost a friggin' husband to cancer. Maybe I wasn't a loser, completely. Maybe I just wanted to find a way to feel better and saw drugs as a way to accomplish this goal. Maybe I am not a terrible person or a fraud. Maybe I just wanted to connect with someone in the same way that I had Michael.

That was the first Thanksgiving that I had spent without Michael. I was further disappointed with the Mel situation, so it's understandable why I did what I did. Not saying that it was the smartest choice, but it did feel like the best option I had for feeling better at the time, and I was desperate.

Now, the second item on the list: Excitement. It reminded me of the connection and excitement I had with Michael and Mel. I wanted to experience that for me. Was that so wrong? Which led to the third item on the menu, which was a reminder of what I had with Michael. Michael and I had a very special love and I had lost that. I wanted to be close with someone. It feels vulnerable to acknowledge that but that is where my random hookups and drugs were stemming from at that time.

As I started dissecting the reasons for what emotional reasons I did the things I did, I started seeing myself as a human being with emotions rather than just someone who needed to do the right thing all the time or get things done. My emotions were more important than accomplishments.

We are now in Chapter 6, but if you look at the history of my life up until this point, you may see a pattern.

My mother felt harassed, so we solved the problem. We moved to The States. I have HIV. Let's solve the problem by adjusting my way of thinking and moving in the direction of being empowered. I couldn't go to college for education. Let's solve the problem by educating myself. Michael is dying. Let's solve the problem by applying holistic solutions.

Had I ever actually taken the time to look at how I felt about having HIV? When I first got diagnosed, my biggest fear was that I was gonna die alone. So, why was it so important for me at that time to have someone to die next to? I wanted to feel loved, honored, worthy, important, significant.

Although I had done the best that I could by giving myself hope for the future, I never addressed what I was yearning for on the inside. I, instead, and I am not judging because I think I did a damn good job with what I had, put my feelings on the back burner and looked toward the future instead. But what about the now of the moment? Just acknowledging what my soul was yearning for changed the way I looked at life completely, along with the way I looked at and dealt with others.

My mother, around this time, was dealing with a string of bad luck that included a car accident, job loss, and a health crisis that all happened at the same time. Mom called me, very upset. Ever the fixer, I gave her solutions. 1) Call insurance and make sure you send them all photos. 2) Get the car fixed and do Uber for a while to supplement income. 3) Go to the doctor and in the meantime take x,y,z supplements.

I heard the disappointment in my mother's voice just before we hung up. At first, I was annoyed. What was her problem? I told her exactly what to do! But then I thought about Abraham Hicks. What had my mother wanted to accomplish by calling me? I put myself in her shoes. If I were her, I might want to call my son because...I want solutions. Okay, since solutions is a noun, what would having solutions give to her emotionally? Assurance. Safety. Understanding. A feeling that she is not in this alone. I called her back.

"Mom. I love you and everything is gonna be okay. I am here with you and we will come up with a solution together. We are family and we support each other. Please know you are not alone. I know you are scared but I have your back."

She broke down into tears as she thanked me. She was so appreciative. We had a long discussion that day and my mother admitted that my problem-solving approach left her feeling as though she were dealing with a manager, not a son. She often felt alone and lonely, as her only family member approached her with a cold clinical analysis that left her empty inside. She wanted an emotional solution not a tactical solution.

It all came together for me one night. I was at home organizing my finances and I realized that I was missing a $3000 check. Where did I put it? I could not find it anywhere! I spun into a tizzy and within minutes found myself crying for Michael. This made a lot of sense since Michael did all of the paperwork/accounting around our home and was the money organizer. I felt vulnerable without his support and completely broke down.

Then, I remembered the emotion principles:

1) At the heart of every desire is the desire to feel

good.

2) (From Jackie) Identify what emotional payoff another person provided and try to give that to yourself.

I took a breath. Okay. I wanted Michael, right now. What did I think I would have emotionally if Michael were here right now? I bawled. LOOOOVEEE. I mean, I was in so much pain but I was crying like Lucy in "I Love Lucy" when Ricky tells her she can't be in the show. I caught a glimpse of myself in the mirror and I could not help but laugh. I mean. I looked kinda funny. Like Sailor Moon when she falls over. I imagined what Michael might say to me if he were in the room.

"C'mon, Baby. Put your big boy pants on. Get it together -- let's gooooo!" Michael was never one to indulge in emotional histrionics.

I continued my thought process. If Michael were in the room right now, what would he say to me? He would tell me everything was alright. Support. Security. Plan. Groundedness. If Michael were in the room during this emotional fit he might first say, "Calm down. No one died." However, since in this case someone (he) had died, he might be nicer about it. I imagined him sitting in the room and talking to me.

"Baby, it's not that big of a deal. It's not the first time you've lost a big check. There is always a solution. We will just reorder the check. You have enough money until the check can be reissued.

Here is a chocolate bar, now come watch Dance Moms with me -- they are gonna start yelling soon."

These fantasies triggered a sense of comfort and

ease and a feeling that everything was going to be okay. So I applied the second half of what I had learned about emotions. I attempted to take on for myself what I had been missing from Michael by talking to myself in similar terms.

"If Mike were here, he would remind me there is a solution. It's just a check. I can reorder it. I've been so strong through all of this -- a $3000 check? Please, c'mon. I lived in the ICU for three months. This is not that serious. Did I check the car?"

Oh my God. In my histrionics I had not yet checked the car. I went to the car, opened the car door, and boom! There it was. The check. I called my friend, Tuesday, to tell her what had just happened. Tuesday, who is one of my friends who sees the value of independence and self-sufficiency, congratulated me on being able to care for myself in this different way. I knew Michael would be proud of me. Most of all, I was so proud of myself. For the first time since Michael's death, I felt that I had taken care of myself emotionally. Not trying to fix a problem with action or a solution, but soothing myself in a way which gave me lasting emotional healing.

Without emotional soothing, I may have found the check, and had the same objective solution. Eventually, I would have looked in the car. But I still would have been left with a deep longing for Michael that I would not know what to do with. This event of emotional care gave me a road map as to how to handle future situations.

Here is another example of this tool in action! Last Christmas, I was going to drive to Seattle to see my mother and spend the holidays with her. I left 10 days empty in my calendar so I could go and see her. Of course, we would inevitably end up at a casino somewhere playing penny slots! It is the Park family tradition to "spend the holidays together" by sitting at different penny slot machines. Once one of us had run out of money to play with, we'd walk around until we'd find a Park with money who could re-fill our bucket. We'd play until we all ran out of money. Good times!

Unfortunately, I miscalculated because this was my mom's first season in Seattle, and it didn't occur to me that the mountainous roads to Washington State would be covered in snow and ice. Not kidding, my first reaction was, "It snows on the West Coast?"

"How are you even alive?" my mom demanded.

She was right. In some ways, I am super-efficient but in some ways I am a total spaz. I guess I just figured the entire west coast was like Los Angeles and like 75 degrees all year round.

I tried to buy plane tickets but they were so expensive because I had waited until the last minute. I told my mom that I didn't think I was gonna make it.

"Oh no!! I was looking forward to having you join us at the casino!" She loves the penny slots casinos. It runs in the family. My grandmother actually requested that her ashes be spread at our nearby Native American casino. Mom and I were going to comply except we found out that it's a felony to spread ashes on reservation grounds. Apparently, we were not the first ones to have the idea. I was secretly relieved because I had this nightmare about how we would spread grandma at the native American casino and she would not be welcome there. What was she gonna say if they try to kick her out? "But I have a player's card!"

So, I was stuck in LA on Christmas Eve. All my friends were pretty much out of town. I was home alone and I started feeling sad. I started getting the pull to go online and find a man to hook up with. In the gay world, it's so easy. Literally, I don't even have to put on socks. Straight guys have to do stuff like leave the house and pay for meals. We gays just flip on the app and decide host or travel! Kidding. Sorta. But anyhow, instead of just following through with this compulsion, I had the mental wherewithal to stop myself this time and ask, "What do you think you will get if you find a hookup?" The answer came to me. "Love. It might remind me of Michael."

Michael. Ugh. Again. I miss the rascal so much. But I proceeded. What is it that I think I will have if Michael were here with me right now? Comfort, family, Christmastime Familiarity. That is actually what came up for me. Actual words from my brain! Okay. What does that mean? Those words represent to me a sense of tradition and warmth and coziness. Ah ha! Now that I have identified what emotions I am trying to get by reaching for Mister Hookup, which is actually Michael, which is actually "Christmas Familiarity," how can I give myself that?

I ordered an extra-large pizza from Michael's and my favorite joint, Masa. Stuffed pizza like you would not believe. With extra cheese. Yum. Great. Then while I waited for the pizza, I went to the 99 Cent Store and shopped for gifts for Michael! Just as a ritual. So I picked up a few items that I thought Michael would like, to honor his memory, picked up the pizza, and came home.

I turned on the TV. One of our traditions was to watch The Amazing Race together. The Amazing Race is a show where teams of two race around the world and have to do things that the local people in various parts of the world do every day. Sometimes, they give you choices about what you can do. "In this detour, the teams may choose between two tasks. In this episode the teams must eat a live scorpion, or circumcise a lion."

Then, of course, the contestants break down and cry while the locals point and laugh and laugh and laugh. In a nutshell, that is the show. Hulu, amazingly (pun intended), had every season of The Amazing Race available to binge online. Perfect! Binging TV shows in front of a massive artery-clogging pizza is just how Michael and I would have spent Christmas!

I set up the gifts I got for Michael on my coffee table and watched The Amazing Race. While playing video games on my phone (which was also tradition), I felt comfy, cozy, and warm. Even though Michael was not there, and it was not quite exactly the same, I got close enough to our traditions to trigger the feelings that I had been craving.

I applied this tool every single time I missed Michael. Actually, I applied this tool every single time I wanted anything! Whenever I felt I wanted, or did not want something, I looked at what I felt the emotional payoff would be if I had the thing that I wanted, and try to find ways to satisfy myself emotionally.

It would not work if I felt too upset, but with steady practice, I reached a noticeable improvement in my emotional stability and well-being, which provided with more energy on my journey to the art of being YAY.

You can leverage your negative emotions to meet your wants and needs!

Flash the QR code below for how!

CHAPTER 7

The Thought Game

I had just played a week in Reno's Comedy Underground with a good friend of mine, Jenny. She is this tall, stunning Latin-American comedian and we would get confused stares every time we walked anywhere.

"What were those two doing together?"

"He looks really gay."

"Oh my, I hope she knows."

So much fun! A fabulous week! All we did was eat buffet, gab, gab, and do fun comedy shows, at which we were both crushing! The comedy club owner that we worked for is a kind and generous man who was very supportive of us and paid for all of our buffet meals. We stayed for hours, using Michael's techniques for breaking even at buffest.

This was in February, so we were getting snow. No one was able to drive in and out of Reno. I was stuck there because I'd driven in before the storm, but my friend had another gig, so I dropped her off at the airport. I drove slowly because I was afraid of the snow. Also, remember,

I am the person who didn't think snow existed west of Colorado. Jenny teased, "You know, you can still push the gas pedal occasionally."

I said, "Better safe than sorry!" We got there but it took 45 minutes to go four miles. We are both alive and that is what matters.

Another 45 minutes after I dropped Jenny off, I was back at the Eldorado Resort Casino. Alone. Snowed in. Sigh. What to do? I turned on the TV. It was like 12 channels of local news and that was it. I contemplated my options. I thought, *I know! I will go on Grindr. Maybe I will meet a cute guy to hang out with.*

Okay, stop judging. I wasn't going to bed with him... necessarily. I thought maybe we could go see a movie or go bowling. Reno proudly hosts the biggest bowling center in the world. Or maybe he could show me around. My favorite movie, *Sister Act*, was filmed there!

Almost immediately, I was hit up by SexyRenoGuy. Actually I don't remember his handle, but it was something like that. I thought he was so hot. Okay, you know how I told you I have a thing for liquor-store-loiterer-looking guys? Well this guy looked like that, except with a blazer, so I thought, *Ah, a reformed liquor store loiterer! Perfect!*

I told him I was staying at the Eldorado. He said he was in the area and would meet me in the lobby in five minutes. I thought, *strange -- his profile says he lives in Reno. Why is he so close to the hotel?*

I went down to the lobby and saw him walk through the door. He walked in wearing dirty wet shoes, an overly worn overcoat with holes in it, and a beanie that looked so discolored from its original red that it looked more like... black-ish? He was so obviously homeless that the Eldorado security guards approached him and said, "Sir, can we help you?"

Oy. I did not know what to do, so in a panic I screamed, "Wait! He's with me!!"

The room fell silent. Everyone in the casino turned around. I don't know why, but all of the machines fell silent also. All the Asian ladies in the casino stared over as if to say, "He's not with us." The security guard nodded in my direction and went back to his post.

SexyRenoGuy stood in front of me. He had no teeth. Then I realized! Duh! While he had been shirtless and showing off in all of the photos, he was never smiling in any of them! Wow! I was still new to the online dating world from having been with Michael for so long that when I told my friend about this topic later, apparently, "it happens all the time" and "you have to ask them to show you their teeth." He still looked like he was in great shape. No teeth. Great abs. I guess they sometimes go hand in hand.

We walked over and sat next to each other in front of penny slot machines. We made small talk, but then he said, "I am so sorry I embarrassed you. It's cold out there. I understand if you don't want to hang out."

Ugh. I felt like such an asshole. I was judging him in my head and I never even bothered to consider how cold a homeless friend would be in the cold. How could I be such a jerk?

I handed him a twenty dollar bill. "This is what my grandma used to do when she would run out of money. She would sit at the machines and play one penny at a time. As long as you are putting money in the machines, they can't kick you out and the waitresses will keep coming around to get you drinks! You can get free drinks all day long!"

He nodded gratefully. I still think about him. I hope he's alright. I hope he won a big jackpot that day.

I got back to my hotel room and I felt like such crap. What a mess. I was judging myself hard. I am awful. I am a mess. I am such a mess. Hadn't I learned my lesson from the roofies incident? Or the Modesto episode? Or Mel? Or -- ughhh. I mean what was wrong with me! I was almost gonna hook up with a homeless guy and I was now low-key judging him for being homeless. What a crap person. Then I took a breath and stopped myself.

Many years ago, I had learned through Neuro-Linguistic Programming seminars that emotions lead to thoughts of a similar tone as the emotions you are feeling, which then trigger an emotion of a similar tone, then thought of the same tone and emotion and on and on and on. In other words, I was about to spiral out.

Knowing the law of emotional and thought momentum, I tried to identify what I was feeling in the hotel room of the Eldorado. Shame. I felt ashamed at feeling uncomfortable with SexyRenoGuy's homelessness. Ashamed at meeting up with a homeless man as my potential date. Just ashamed. I felt like a mess.

I went online and once again consulted The Almighty Google. First search result: Feeling Shame? Lonely? Call Dr. Xyz now for a free consultation (Sponsored Ad).

Ugh. Next! Affirmations.

"I am awesome."

"I am awesome."

"I am awesome."

(Not feeling better.) "I AM AWESOME!"

"I AM AWESOME!"

"SHUUUT UP, NEGATIVE MIND -- I AM AWESOME!!"

(Now I'm a messy person who is also hysterical.) "I am AWESOME!!!"

"I am AWESOME!!!"

After a little while of this, I ended up feeling like even more of a mess. Not only did I feel like a mess, I now felt like I was a hysterical mess, and a liar, who also sucks at affirmations. Whatever I was doing was clearly not working. I walked into the bathroom to wash my face, mostly because that's what they do in movies. Then I saw my HIV pill bottle. I had left the bottle open. which was not like me.

First I thought, "Is there a ghost in this hotel room?" Jenny and I had hung out in the room the night before and she told me that she felt a presence. OMG. What if there is a ghost at the Eldorado?

Then, for some reason, I was reminded of Mark, the therapist intern who had made me feel better about the HIV situation. I had walked into the office thinking I was gonna die alone, and I walked out feeling like there was a possibility for a great life.

Then it clicked!

The reason why Mark's approach had worked for me was that when I presented Mark with my fear of dying alone, he acknowledged that it was possible that it could happen, but also there were lots of people with HIV who did not die alone. He gave me something that I could actually believe, as opposed to a dogma or a statement to recite as programming.

Instead of, "You are not going to die alone, Aidan," which I would have not been able to believe at the time, Mark offered an alternative belief. "You might die alone... but there are people who live good lives with HIV."

I realized that the reason affirmations were not working for me was because I was not in the space to believe them. Repeating affirmations to myself that I didn't believe felt kind of like stapling index cards to my head and getting frustrated at the fact that I was in pain and bleeding. It's a bloody mess for the hard-headed. The key was to try to find an alternative belief that was less negative than what I was currently thinking but was true.

I tried.

"I'm awesome?"

Ooh. Nope. That felt like a lie. Let's try again.

"I suck at this."

True, but that didn't move me in the direction of feeling more positive. What is the alternative thought that makes me feel better, that I can believe from where I stand?

"I make okay decisions some of the time -- and -- I am not always a mess."

Huh. Okay I could actually believe this thought. Because it is true! Who can refute this statement? Who doesn't make okay decisions some of the time? I also agree with the second half of the statement. I am not a mess "all of the time." Even the craziest ex-teen mom reality stars have their moments. Okay. So. Great! I could work with this statement.

Then I remembered what I did to strengthen my belief once I found out about the potential for HIV positive people being able to lead good lives! I Googled for evidence! I also did the same with successful people who never completed college. So, if the principle worked the same way, I would have to take this softer belief that I could actually take on as truthful and provide evidence for it!

I took out my journal, flipped to a blank page, and wrote across the top:

Evidence for how I make okay decisions some of the time and I am not always a mess.

I paused. I was still upset so it was hard to come up with something that I had done right. I started to wonder if I was kidding myself with this exercise. Then I got inspired. Gasp! I wrote down my first piece of evidence:

1. This may or may not work but at least by doing this exercise I am showing that I am trying to take care of my emotions, which is proactive.

Ah! Very good! It's true! By doing the exercise and actively thinking about my situation in the hopes of a better feeling, I was making a good choice! I mean sure I didn't know whether this was actually going to work, but at least I was trying! I could have gone online and found another guy and -- ooh! There is another one.

2. I could be online looking for another guy. Instead, I am reflecting.

Also true! That's kind of cool, reflecting to improve my well-being over looking for a random hookup is certainly the behavior of someone who makes good decisions some of the time! Wow. Okay....Then I started laughing at myself.

3. I didn't bring the homeless guy upstairs.

Very proud of that one! I mean, someone who is a complete mess might have brought him upstairs but I gave him twenty bucks and…OMG.

4. I didn't say, "screw you" and leave him in the dust. I gave him $20 so he can stay warm!

That was nice! I mean I was not Mother Teresa or anything but considering I was $15,000 in debt with another $30,000 in auto loans at the time this happened -- which technically meant the homeless guy was probably richer than me -- I did what I could to make sure he was okay for a while. Could I have done better? Maybe. Did I do okay? At least a C-. Cs get degrees.

I was on a roll.

5. I had a great weekend at a comedy club and got a lot of laughs so I must be doing something right.

6. I am warm and healthy.

7. I can experience an event like this and not end up completely inconsolable, due to practicing care for my emotional well-being.

I examined the list. Wait. This list looked pretty damn good. This looked like the list of someone who made good decisions a good amount of times, and is a mess only rarely! Huh!

So then I started a new page:

Evidence for how I make good decisions a good amount of times and am a mess only rarely.

The first thing that popped into my head was the incident at Modesto. Yikes. I felt bad about it. I started feeling myself move down, then I wrote down.

1. Even though the Modesto event was not great, I used that opportunity to leverage a better choice for next time.

That is a true statement that no one could refute. I absolutely examined what happened that day and tried to make a better choice. NO, I was not perfect, but....

2. I am looking in the direction of beating myself up less and affirming the good things that I have done.

3. I feel better and I can see a strategy for me that is actually working.

4. If Michael saw this, I think he would approve.

5. Mark the Intern would definitely approve.

6. I approve because I feel better than I did just a few minutes ago.

So, at this moment, I learned that when I am in a negative spiral, I don't want to mindlessly chant unbelievable affirmations. I want to make a statement that I cannot refute, but also moves me in the direction of positivity. Then provide evidence for why that belief is true until that becomes the new normal.

I started applying this technique to other areas that I felt vulnerable about. One area was money. I was $15,000 in debt from credit card bills and at the time it felt insurmountable to overcome. How could I get out of such high interest credit card debt, when I was so knee deep? I went back to the page.

Old Thought: I will never get out of this credit card debt.

New Thought: There are lots of people who have successfully paid off credit card debt.

Test: Did this thought lead me to more optimism? Yes. Is this statement irrefutable? Yes.

Now the evidence:

My friend Emily.

My friend Johnny.

Joan Rivers had $250 million dollars in debt at one point, did she not?

Duh! Me! Just a few years ago, I had a financial situation and I paid off $7,000 in a matter of 3 months by taking on contract jobs!

I continued this exercise until the evidence for the second, more positive, belief was so overwhelming that it overshadowed the first one. (I am debt free now, by the way.)

In the upcoming weeks, I approached my life with the attitude of refusing to take negative beliefs about myself at face value, but making it a habit of examining myself through the eyes of a more optimistic truth.

I take great pride in my work. I like to think I am hilarious, so I was excited to be booked as a host for a major comedy club Las Vegas. What a great opportunity! I was tremendously excited to be playing this prestigious venue, but I ran into a hiccup.

After a week of hosting, the comedy club owner pulled me into his office for a meeting. "Aidan, I am very disappointed. I had such high hopes for you. You were not that funny this week. I don't think you are funny enough to play this club again."

WOW. This is a comedian's worst nightmare. I asked him what he felt was the problem.

"There are not enough jokes," he replied. "You are rambling, and I want top quality jokes. Like you did in your audition. I don't know what happened to you."

I almost dissolved into tears right then and there. I was so proud and excited to have been playing this prestigious club in Viva Las Vegas and here I was being told I was not funny enough to come back.

"You have a good look, though," he said.

Gee, thanks. He was right, I looked damn good. But apparently, my comedy sucked. I felt confused and insulted. However, I was not going to take this negative belief and spiral.

I sat in my hotel room, about to call a friend to vent about what happened, but I decided to stop myself and look at the situation. Given the circumstances, it would be easy for any comedian to travel to the Land of Negative Thoughts:

I suck.

I should quit.

I am a loser.

My career is a lie.

And so on and so on and so on. With the laws of emotional-and-thought momentum at play, I could also easily go down a rabbit hole of negativity very quickly. Calling my friend would have only accelerated my spiral as I vented and added momentum to the negative emotion.

Instead I stopped myself and did the process:

Belief: I am a terrible comedian and I should quit.

More Optimistic Belief that is Undeniably True: A lot of people really like my comedy.

The second belief was a bit of a reach from where I was emotionally because I had just received the news of disapproval. So I picked one that was even easier to believe.

I picked: Some people really like my comedy.

*Evidence…*Immediately, I started arguing with myself. This is hopeless, no one who has control over the booking of any important shows likes my comedy. Then, I laughed at the fatalistically absurd statement. The owners of huge comedy clubs in Hollywood trusted me enough to perform weekly, in 20-minute chunks, for the past five years! So, right there!

1. Many comedy clubs in Hollywood and the team there really like and support my comedy.

It's true! I mean, actually, sometimes there have been bookers there who did not prefer my comedy, and while they were in charge I got fewer bookings, but that happens to pretty much every comedian who has been in the business a while.

2. I get DMs from fans every day who tell me how

much they love my comedy.

This one was true as well!

3. Michael loved my comedy. He didn't know how to lie. He would have told me. In fact, he would always tell me when I bombed.

4. Mel was impressed with my comedy.

I mean, I was dating the guy, so I think you get extra points when you do stuff with them, but he did see me before we entered a committed relationship and....

5. This other comedy club owner actually called me last week to tell me that I was her favorite comedian she's ever had come through the club.

So, maybe a lot of people like my comedy and I don't have to be for everyone. In fact, I realized at that point that I actually love my comedy! I love my comedy, and so do a lot of people and I don't have to be for everyone. It took a day or two to reinforce this belief, considering the traumatic event that had just occurred, but I kept going until my funniness was no longer in question.

I realized, even the booker who criticized me said he liked my audition. So, what happened? Since I was no longer emotionally wrapped up in the event, I could examine his critique from a neutral place. For the audition, I brought as many jokes as I possibly could fit into each minute of comedy, whereas during the week, I focused more on making the audience comfortable by taking it slower and talking to them. In trying to do my job in the way that I thought was most appropriate, I was not matching what the comedy booker wanted, which was less audience work, and more jokes per minute.

Even though I had received a negative review, I had one day of the gig left. So I went back to the hotel room, revised my comedy routine, and delivered the product that the comedy booker wanted. The booker was not in the room that night, however the headliner of the week's show noticed a huge difference in the amount of laughs I got. Because the comedy booker was not in the room, I don't know how much good it actually did in regard to being invited back for the future shows at said club. However, I have never been more proud of a good set because it resulted from an active engagement of the tools I had developed for a happier life.

That is when I realized that we are so inclined toward the negative in this world. It's so much easier to say "I sucked" versus "I was great." Why? I am not sure, but I hear 10 times the number of people who might say something like, "I am dumb" versus "I am smart." I think it is autopilot that we just kind of fall into because we don't want to make anyone feel uncomfortable or insecure. We are taught to keep our heads down and not put ourselves out there too much. So we downplay who we are, and pretty soon we start to believe our own language.

I said in the first chapter that I am one of the happiest people that people meet and I think it is a direct result of my positive opinion of myself that I have crafted by doing the processes in the book and also acknowledging my desires and taking care of myself emotionally.

Never mind the opinion of the comedy booker, or anyone else in the world, I think I am funny. I have enough evidence to show that I am funny. I am a strong individual. I am a solid individual who has displayed a lot of grit, determination and rigor in my approach to life. I am a good person. I want to be kind to others and want to encourage other people to be/feel the best that they can.

I really think that a positive opinion of myself and my belief that I will be able to handle whatever comes my way, a belief about myself that I have instilled through The Thought Game outlined in this chapter, is why I am indeed positive. My opinion of myself is pretty damn good! Why not! I am awesome!

Remember when I said, "I am awesome" in my affirmation? Well, I could not believe that I was so awesome at the time, but nowadays I feel that I am pretty damn awesome. It started with, "I make good decisions sometimes." Once I got strong enough in that belief, I was able to take on the next level up belief of, "I make good decisions a lot of the time." Then, once I got strong enough in that belief and felt I had enough evidence to truly take it on as my truth, I took on, "I may not be perfect but I am doing very well" -- which soon turned into, "I am pretty damn awesome, and who the hell is perfect all the time? I'm awesome."

I found this tool to be so effective that every time I started getting a negative thought about myself, I would sit down and write an alternative belief. One that I could not refute and that made me feel better or hopeful about the future. Then I would write evidence for the alternate belief until I felt strong enough about it that it felt like my truth, then I would move on to an even stronger belief that I felt I could adopt as my truth! Through deliberate practice, I changed my frame of mind on the following topics:

Negative thought: I am ugly and fat (remember I was

a chubby kid),

More positive and believable thought: Some people think I'm very attractive, and I also think this some of the time.

Next level more positive and believable thought: A lot of people find me attractive. I also like many elements of who I am physically. I am tall and strong, with dark features. I don't look half bad.

Next level up: I like the way I look and I may not be for everyone but I think I look pretty damn good. I am proud of the way I look.

This takes, like, four-to-five days of deliberate exercise of thought, in like, 15-minute spurts of thought exercise. After about three months of active practice, my opinion about myself completely turned around. I took on negative beliefs about myself and things about myself I wanted to change. I'll do this exercise with a few things I took on as examples.

Old Belief: I am disorganized.

New Belief: I am not currently as organized as I would like to be, right now, but I can learn to get better at it, and I am working in that direction.

Now you must ask yourself two questions.
1) Is the new belief More optimistic/positive than the old belief?
2) Is the new belief totally believable?
If the answers to these two questions are yes, then you can move on to the evidencing!

Evidence:

I am learning to pick up trash as I move about the apartment and it is a habit that I can see instilling in myself.

I see the value of being more organized, which I hadn't noticed before since Michael was in charge of the cleaning of the home.

Sometimes, I enjoy the organization process; it feels meditative.

I just watched 12 episodes of Marie Kondo so I must have picked up a thing or two through osmosis, if not consciously, right?

The old belief became: I am not currently as organized as I would like to be, right now, but I can learn to get better at it, and I am working in that direction. Which allowed for my new belief.

New Belief: I am doing a good job being more organized.

Evidence:

I just Marie Kondo'd my closet, so I know I learned something.

My mom just came over and literally said, "WOW. No socks on floor -- Whuuuuh?"

I just swept 10 minutes ago, like it was a routine. I didn't think about it.

Pretty soon.. I was a thought-turning machine.

I have a terrible temper -- into -- I have pretty good emotional control and I am getting better all the time.

I'm broke -- into -- I may not be wealthy right now, but I have everything it takes to make a lot of money.

There is something wrong with me -- into -- No one is perfect. I like who I am, for the most part.

I found that this technique also works on regrets. I was so hard on Michael in the last days of his life. I wish I could have focused more on making him comfortable and providing ease rather than treating him like an NFL quarterback who was refusing to go onto the football field.

I used to sit in shame often and say, "I am sorry Michael. I was wrong and I hope I didn't make your life too hard in your last days." In the dark, with the lights off, like I was in some kind of hipster arthouse film. Koreans are dramatic, I told you!

I decided to take on my shame in the exact same way I had my other negative beliefs.

Old Belief: I suck as a partner for what I did to Mike.

New Belief: I was doing my best.

This, I can say, was absolutely true. I was doing my best. I just really wanted him to live and I wanted to feel as though we were fighting together. In retrospect, of course, just like a coach on the football team, I was merely giving advice from the sidelines. All the heavy lifting and battling was done by the athlete. It is the athlete that has to suffer the physical fatigue/injuries and it was unfair for me to yell at him to do better.

Despite my wrongheaded approach, I did do my best.

Evidence:

Everything I did, I did because I thought it would bring him closer to victory over his cancer.

No cost was spared.

I would have died for that man.

I started getting teary-eyed. I was so deep into my shame that I had never taken the time to consider how I was feeling during the process. I would have died for him, if I could have. Honestly. There are many nights when I would pray, "Lord, can you just take me?" I am not sure if it was motivated by my desire to save him or by my fear of being left behind. But if someone had given me a red button to push that would have let me trade places with him, I would have. In a heartbeat.

This new way of thinking allowed me to own that I was wrongheaded in my approach to Michael's cancer. But it also allowed me to acknowledge that I did the best I could. I was not trying to harm anyone.

This brought me to the topic of Grandma. Big jump. I know, but stay with me.

My grandmother died without ever knowing that I was gay. I mean, at this point you may be wondering, "Aidan, was she deaf and blind?" Well, you know, there is no gay in Korea. Truly there is not. I mean there might be gay now but at the time that Grandma left Korea, there was not such a thing as "Gay." Like, in Korea, they would bring the musical Rent in and legit make Angel a woman (as opposed to a trans woman, as is originally written) to take out any controversies.

When my grandmother moved to the United States and discovered gayness, she was shocked and appalled! She had never thought of such a thing. Grandma was a very religious woman, devoted to her spirituality and her life of

Christianity. She found homosexuality to be a sin. Period.

I think that it would be pretty easy for me to be hurt by her perspective and call her "short-sighted and hypocritical." I mean, there kinda were those aspects to her that were hypocritical. Like, she would read The Bible every single morning and then later on in the day she would ask if we could go to the casino. She had a free buffet coupon and of course she wasn't going to actually gamble -- three hours later she would have lost $400 on penny slots. Aww... Grandma, I miss you!

But here is the reality of the situation. Grandma's religiousness hurt me (unbeknownst to her) because I never felt that she would ever accept me for who I was. But if I can honor myself and my behavior with Michael as someone who was trying their best, I could also honor Grandma as someone who was trying her best with what she knew. She didn't have a lot of money, she never had an education. She didn't really have much to live for. All she had left to hold on to was a good turnout for me and Mom, and a wonderful Afterlife in which she would get a chance to become the woman she always wanted to be!

Grandma was domestically abused, lived through two wars, raised five children in Korea and supported them while Grandpa was out gambling, went through bankruptcies and, oh, so much.... She then moved to the United States with the hopes of a better life for me and my mother. From that perspective, I can be grateful that Grandma had found a religion that provided her so much. Anything that threatened her faith had to be dismissed because the hope her faith provided was essential to her survival!

If you asked me now, I would say I am very glad that

Grandma found religion, despite her dogmatic approach. Grandma found a great deal of comfort from having her spiritual practice. I would also say that I benefited because it gave me an opportunity to learn how to stand in the truth of who I am in harsh conditions. She did much for me and mom and I am so grateful that she did the best that she could do.

At the end of the day, as she was saying her goodbyes, I didn't feel the need to tell her I was gay. I didn't need to prove myself right. I just wanted to thank her for the love that she had for us. I choose to believe that she had a heart of gold and did the best she could with what she knew and what was available to her. She also wanted all of us to be Christian because it brought her so much comfort and peace, and she wanted that for us too.

We all seem to walk through life with so much shame about our pasts and judgement of others but this thought method really helped me see that, indeed, we are all hurt people doing the best that we can. Even though our tactics may be wrongheaded or even damaging, most of us are doing our best. It gives me great relief to look at life in this way because, again, it is a true statement that moves me in the direction of feeling better about myself, and the world at large. We get to choose the truth we would like to hold and instead of just taking whatever we feel first at face value, I say one of the key ingredients in the art of being YAY is deliberately choosing to pick the belief that is not only true, but also advantageous to you and your well-being.

How to improve your self esteem using the concepts in this chapter!

Flash the QR code below for a video on how!

CHAPTER 8:

Deeper Into the Thought Game

It was summer of 2019 and I missed Mel. Why? Why? Why could I not stop thinking about this man that I knew was so bad for me? So I turned on Dua Lipa who has a song called, "New Rules." It's about her getting screwed over by some F-boy again and again and she finally gets sick of it so she wrote a song about the advice that she shares with her girlfriends when they encounter F-Boys.

Don't pick up the phone, you know he's calling cause he's drunk and alone.

Don't let him in, you'll have to kick him out again.

Don't be his friend, you know you are gonna wake up in his bed in the morning. If you are under him, you ain't getting over him.

The ironic thing was, he was not calling, he was not asking to come over, and he was not asking to be my friend -- but the song is great nonetheless, and made me feel empowered. After about five listens, I decided I had had enough and examined why I missed Mel. I missed Mike. Of course. I mean, to be fair, Mel resembled Michael closer than any other man in my life -- and Mel was alive. So, since Michael was off chillaxing with Jesus, I wanted to call Mel.

Then I examined further, using the tools from the past two chapters. What is the feeling that I think I will have if I have Michael here? I realized that on that particular day, I missed the sense of excitement and anticipation I felt when Michael and I had a vacation coming up. Once a month, we would pack our bags, pick a random location, and drive there. We would spend the entire day just having a good time with one another.

One of our favorite destinations was Joshua Tree. The area was colorful and strange; full of dirt, thrift stores, and hippie art stores. But also there is a Walmart, a Target, and a Panda Express. Joshua Tree is a strange world, but one we thought was interesting and cool.

Once I identified what I was actually craving, I decided to give myself that sense of adventure. Michael was not coming back and it would not have been fair to myself or to Mel if I were to dial up Mel so he could replace Mike.

I drove to Joshua Tree, listening to my favorite tunes and arrived at an Airbnb that I had booked on a whim. I walked into the most awesome-looking home; a mix of mid-century modern and desert paradise. It looked like something out of an architecture magazine. So cool!

I spent two days shopping, eating at all the cool looking restaurants, walking around the scenic areas of Joshua Tree National Park, and meeting the locals. Maria, a Mother of two from Denny's. Jennifer, who worked at the local real estate company and described the drama between all of the real estate companies. Apparently, it's a real dog-eat-dog world in the landscape of Joshua Tree real estate. My favorites were Ann and Rabe, this couple I met at the Dollar General, who had been living in Joshua tree for 20 years and complained about gentrification.

I was having the best time until I woke up on the third morning with a raised bump on my upper thigh. I mean, it was huge. Red and swollen with a bite mark in the center. Super not cute. Then I started poking at it. It was warm to the touch. What was it? I thought it was one of those situations where in this one movie this girl has a pimple and her face explodes and all these spiders come out of there!

Naturally, I went on Facebook to contact my nurse friend and hilarious comedian, Michelle. I sent her a photo. In seconds she said, "Go to the ER. It's either infected or it is a tick bite that if left untreated could develop into Lyme Disease." I knew that Shania Twain had Lyme disease that made her lose control of her voice, which is why she had to step down as America's (or Canada's) Country Crossover Sweetheart for a few years. I didn't want to lose my voice. I am the karaoke champ! I could not bear it!

So, I went to the ER. I signed in and sat in the waiting room. I felt negative feelings welling up inside of me. I had driven to Joshua Tree in order to give myself what I had missed in my lost lover. Joshua Tree was a place that the two of us treasured and here I was alone and scared, in the Emergency Room.

I thought, *I try to be nice to myself and look what happened. This sucks. There is no hope. I miss Michael. If Michael were here, I would have someone here with me. I would not be alone. I wouldn't have to work so damn hard to feel okay. Screw my life. I give up.*

I stopped myself. *Whoa, horsie -- cool it!* I recognized the beginning stages of negative thought momentum. I decided to look for an alternative thought about the situation that would be more empowering/hopeful and ring true for where I was. In the same way that I had done with the beliefs about myself, I was hoping to optimize my point-of-view of the current situation.

Thought: I tried to do good for myself, and it's all hopeless. Look where I am. In the Emergency Room. This is what I get for trying to do my best.

What could be an alternative and also true thought that was about the event?

New Thought: At least, I have insurance and can take care of this.

Okay. This is true. Then I noticed that I had just said, can take care of this. Something about that statement gave me joy. So I created another thought.

New thought: At least I am taking care of myself.

I liked that thought and I thought it rang true so I went for the evidence.

Evidence:

Michael is not here and I brought myself into the hospital, which is self-care.

It didn't quite turn out the way I planned but I am taking good care of myself, or at least attempting to.

I didn't need much evidence before I realized that I had a choice to look at the current situation any way I wanted to look at it. I chose the I-can-take-care-of-myself-and-I-am-proud-of-me, narrative over the life-is-hopeless narrative, only because I wanted to feel good. Somewhere along the line in my search of YAY, my priorities had shifted. In the beginning, I was determined to stop feeling bad. Now, I wanted to start feeling good.

I realized that while I was in the Emergency Room, I was not only taking care of myself physically by bringing myself to the hospital, I was also taking care of myself mentally by finding evidence for a positive attitude toward my situation.

I looked around the Emergency Room and spotted a little Latina girl who had come in because her ears hurt. She was surrounded by family members. I saw the warmth and the love that the family was pouring on this girl, and the gratitude and relief she felt as she watched a children's show on her iPad and sucked on a lollipop.

I remembered being taken to the emergency room in Korea when I was a child and my mom and my grandmother both being there for me. They loved me so much and it made me feel grateful to have had a wonderful childhood wherein I was protected and loved by two amazing women.

I looked at myself at that moment; a man in his 30's who had taken himself into the Emergency Room and thought, *Well damn. I turned out okay. If I can be proud of myself and feel empowered during an emergency room visit, less than a year after the death of my husband. Damn. Good job to the Park family and good job to Aidan.*

I looked at the little girl and thought, *She's so cute. I hope that she grows up continuing to be surrounded by love. One day she might have to take herself to the ER. If she does, I hope that she will feel as empowered as I do right now about it.*

In reflection of that thought, just for fun, I looked for possible negative attitudes I could have held about that girl and her family in the ER. I thought, *well, she us surrounded by a family that loves her and I am not.* It was then I realized that I had been able to look at the girl and her family in the spirit of empowered gratitude because I was already in a positive state of emotion when I first observed the family.

This observation further strengthened my belief in emotional momentum. The girl and her family were going to be in the emergency room regardless of how I was going to feel about it. But my feelings about the girl and the family would be determined by my emotional state as an observer. It would have been pretty much guaranteed that if I had walked into the emergency room with the attitude of, *I am lonely and sad Michael is not here and it's hopeless*, then saw the girl and family, it would have given momentum to my loneliness.

That was such a cool discovery. As I was contemplating this, the doctor came to examine my giant tick bite. Which led to a conversation that went something like this…

Doctor (examining the tick bite): You are gonna be fine. We will give you an antibiotic to clear this up. I will write you a prescription. By the way, have you been to the East Coast lately?

Me: Uh.. no?

Doctor: (now poking at the tick bite) Well this tick bite

is actually a bite from a rare kind of tick that only actually exists on the East Coast. How did this happen?

Me: Uh -- I don't know?

Doctor: This is so unusual.

Okay. This is another weird moment where I could choose whatever I wanted to think about it. I could think. Well, screw my life. How unlucky does one have to be to not only get a tick bite but manage to get a tick from the East Coast? But since I was in a momentum of positivity, I just joked around with him.

Me: Maybe he's a New Yorker.

We both burst out laughing.

Doctor: I know this is weird but would you mind if I called some of my colleagues over and showed them what a real life tick bite looks like from this particular tick? We never see it on the West Coast.

Me. (pause) Sure, C'mon, it's a party! Bring the children. I got nowhere to go, but I'd like a lollipop.

They gave me a lollipop and the doctors came in three at a time to "ooh" and "ahh" over my tick bite. I made jokes about how I would be much happier if I got this much attention for my upper thigh from doctors all the time. The doctors were grateful for having seen this… uhh.. modern marvel? But I could tell the experience also brought some levity to their stressful day.

I walked out with my prescriptions and contemplated the good time that I shared with the doctors. The good time I had was a direct result of the positive attitude that I had deliberately taken. If I were a patient who looked upset, the doctor certainly would not have joked around with me, or even asked me if he could invite colleagues to touch my leg. He saw that I could emotionally handle the request and it left an opening for an experience I could laugh about with my friends for years to come.

I called my friend Kate (hilarious comedian and soul sister) to tell her what had happened. I told her how proud I was of my active decision-making, of the little girl, of the doctors feeling me up. She was ecstatic for me and shared in my sentiment that Michael would have been so proud and that she was also proud of me for being so active in my search for happiness.

Again, I contemplated what might have happened in reverse, had I chosen a different framing around the same events. Had I decided to remain in the negative thought pattern, I might have seen the girl and felt negatively, would not have had a good interaction with the doctor, and I don't think I would have walked out with any lollipops (which I ended up getting two of). Then I would have called Kate in the parking lot and presented a very different story.

"Kate, I took myself to the hospital and got a tick bite, and now I am alone and sad in this town. And they didn't even give me a lollipop!"

Being the good friend that I know Kate to be, I know exactly what she would have said to me. "Aidan, I am so sorry. It's alright. It's understandable that you feel sad. I love you and I am here for you."

I am lucky enough to have friends who will be there for me no matter what but the type of support would mirror my attitude toward the event. As I presented an empowered attitude toward my trip to the ER, Kate reflected support for the empowered attitude. In the alternate universe, an attitude of self-pity would have call for consolation rather than congratulations.

This was very much like the incident from Chapter 2 where I got HIV. The search terms I typed into Google were what the engine used to calibrate my results. Are HIV positive people lonely? Boom, search results for HIV positive people. Are there successful and happy people with HIV? Boom, successful people with HIV who are happy.

Around this time, I was in a hit-and-run accident. After obeying a stop sign like a good boy, this red pickup truck sped down the road and smashed into me, pretty damn hard. Then without getting out of the truck, sped off as quickly as he could.

I pulled over to the side of the road and my passenger side door was completely crushed in. I was annoyed. I had been on my way home to eat my delicious double chicken salad from El Pollo Loco. People walking by with sympathetic head shakes felt more embarrassing than supportive.

I called Geico. The representative showed up, took notes, and sent me to the auto shop where they had taken my car. I ate my salad in the waiting room. I felt my annoyance rising, so I decided to play The Thought Game.

I ran into a speed bump, though. I felt like I was absolutely within my rights to get angry at the driver and the world because I had done nothing wrong! What had I done to deserve a hit-and-run? I was the victim here! Screw that loser with his pickup truck from the 1980's. Life is unfair. I paused. Huh. I went from the it- was-that-guy's-fault narrative, to the life-is-unfair narrative so quickly.

One of the first lessons that I had learned in researching success principles in my late teens, was to take responsibility for everything in my life. For example, even though I had taken on the possibility of being successful with HIV and without a college degree, when I hit age 21, my anger at life really boiled over. I was angry at the world. It just seemed so unfair.

Why did I have to work so much harder than everyone else? Why did I have no parenting other than my (loving but) Christian grandmother who thought gays were going straight to Hell? Why did I have no money? Why was I not finding success in my career that I wanted so badly? Why was I not born more beautiful? Why couldn't I go to college when I worked so hard to get into great schools? Why did I get HIV? Why me?

Not that I didn't have good reason to feel the way I felt. I had friends who were going to college and about to graduate from schools that I should have been able to go to! Many of my friends were entering the work force in positions that were paying four or five times what I was making at Starbucks when I was 22 years old (I had gotten permanent residence by then).

It was scary how quickly anger transitioned into anxiety, which then transitioned into hopelessness. I stopped trying. I resigned myself to a life of mediocre hourly work, and to a life of discontent, and I kind of -- stopped.

I struggled to wake up in the morning. When I would see myself in the mirror, I would think, *Ugh, it's you again*. Then I would look at my face in disgust. I would take a shower before plopping on my couch to watch all the successful, pretty people live their lives. I ate, derided myself for being fat, and bemoaned that I was not born with better self-control. I found myself pathetic and disgusting. I looked at my shoes that were falling apart and ragged clothing and bemoaned the fact that I was poor. I bemoaned that I was not more talented. Then I blamed my mom for not telling me I was undocumented, earlier, so I could avoid this life of misery.

I let my healthcare slip. I had all of the resources available to me but eventually stopped going to see the doctor for my HIV. My depression combined with my lack of care created an environment for my health to decline very quickly. I started getting sick. I would get colds that would last literally 2-3 months. Great. Illness. I found even more reasons to be angry at life.

My boyfriend at the time, worried, kept telling me to go to the doctor, but I ignored him because I was simply too sad to take charge of my life. Besides, what would be the point of this? Why did I even want to be alive in this chaotic world that I could not control? I thought I was a loser for not having figured it out. I thought I was unlucky for my misfortunes. I thought I was ugly and untalented. A pipe dreamer with no hope. I was powerless to my loser personality and to my misfortunes....

I ended up with pneumonia and was forced to see a doctor. Okay, here's the thing about HIV; you have these things called T cell counts. My doctor asked if I had been taking my medications because My T cell count was in the high 300s. An undiagnosed person would have a T cell of around 800-1200. It's considered AIDS if you have less than 200. I was close to having AIDS due to my own lack of self-care.

That scared the crap out of me. Then the doctor asked me why I hadn't been to see a doctor in almost a year and why I was not on any medications when so many programs were available to me to take advantage of…. Good point, Doc.

Why hadn't I taken charge of my own well-being? Why hadn't I sought the support that was available to me? At first I thought, *why do I have to do all the work?* Then reality hit. Who else would do the work for my well-being if I were not willing to take the help that was offered? I mean, what were these people supposed to do? Barrel down the door to make sure I was doing okay? Get a net and take me away like they do in the Looney Tunes cartoons?

I was the one holding myself back from all of the wonderful help that was available to me because I was living in the thick of thoughts that were not serving me. Just like in the situations with the guy who roofied me and the hit-and-run driver. Yes, it's natural to be angry and hurt when something fucked-up happens. We should definitely acknowledge and validate those feelings, but we can't nurture and feed them, or they only get stronger. We can't control the past but we can choose what we build our futures on; dark clouds or silver linings.

In 2006, when confronted with why I had not been more active in my self-care, I blamed everything outside. I pointed to…

1) My being a loser. (Was this true? Was it a truth I

had built without knowing what I was doing? Didn't I have any reasons to think that I was a decent person? The answer is, I DID.)

2) My being poor. (What does this have to do with taking advantage of free resources?)

3) My being unlucky. If I hadn't gotten HIV due to my shitty environment then I would not be here… (OK maybe I had been unlucky, so now what? Did it serve me to just define myself as unlucky and live my life as such?)

4) My Grandma's lack of understanding of gay culture?

5) My undocumented status?

I am not beating up on myself for feeling what I felt at the time. My point is that it was not serving me and I could have been happier had I actively applied what I know now. Blame is the act of giving power away. If my happiness is reliant on other people or my circumstances, the world has to comply with the conditions I require in order to be happy. The only problem with that is that the world rarely cares about my happiness. I can't control what happens around me. I can only appreciate the good and use the tools I've cultivated in order to deal with the bad.

When I was 21, my doctor asked me very pointedly why I hadn't been going to the doctor. I could have said, "I didn't come to the doctor because I am sad because I am a loser and poor and unlucky and my grandmother doesn't love me and I am undocumented." But what did that actually have to do with my check-ups? Not much. But I could certainly link it and feel justified in my sadness and not have to take responsibility for my emotions by blaming things outside of myself.

At that point, I decided to buckle down and change my life. I made myself work out every day, get up and do the things I meant to do, and really get motivated. Which was not a bad approach. But from the perspective where I am sitting right now, I think there was a better way. I understand that I was "buckling down" in pursuit of a better feeling. I realize now that I didn't need to improve my conditions in order to enjoy good feelings. I could have had good feelings all along the way.

I could have decided to actively be appreciative of the healthcare services available to me. For the opportunity I had working at Starbucks with co-workers who were kind and loving to me. For my grandmother and mother who loved me unconditionally. For my boyfriend at the time, Bart, who loved me deeply and who I am grateful to have had in my life, even to this day. For Bart's cat Willie, this crazy needy cat who thought he was a dog and would meow until you petted him. (Willie had a twin brother, Hank, who ran away, so I think Willie was emotionally damaged. Aren't we all?)

Looking back on when I was 21, there truly was much to be excited and grateful for, and there was also much to be angry about. I just didn't know how to activate specific emotions, yet. I did the best I could and I certainly am not judging myself. In writing this book and putting my life down on paper, I can see that, dayum! I am a soldier. That said, being young would have been more fun if I'd have had the ability to choose my emotional tones, rather than waiting for my conditions to improve.

I am 100% right to think that I am a victim of an

unfortunate circumstance in Michael's death. I am within my rights to feel sad. Angry. Envious of others who have not experienced similar losses. And I felt all of those things. But I pretty quickly got sick of suffering. I reached a point where I knew that I had a right to feel sad, but did not want to.

So, as I sat in the waiting room of the auto body shop, I knew that even though I was within my rights to play the victim, as I was literally the victim of a hit-and-run, that the narrative of being powerless over the situation would not serve me. So, playing The Thought Game again, we have:

The first thought that struck me was: My life sucks and I am unlucky.

Better thought that is also believable: I am lucky because I can afford to deal with this.

Evidence:

I can actually pay for this with cash. Awesome.

Geico came so fast.

I'm getting a rental and I am eating my salad. All is good.

Then I started getting thoughts about the driver who hit me.

Thought: What an asshole.

Better thought that is also believable: The driver maybe was not in the space to be able to afford taking responsibility for a hit-and-run.

Evidence:

His car was a red pickup from the 1980s. It was old.

He wasn't rolling in dough.

A $1,000 deductible to him could have been the difference between rent or no rent. He might have a family to feed.

Maybe he was undocumented? I mean, if I was undocumented, I would have been scared to have the police be called on me. If I had hit someone under those circumstances, I might have done the same thing.

Now, I don't actually know if any of those things are true. But from what I knew about the guy driving the red truck, my made-up evidence is as valid as thinking, *he is a drug addict on the run and doesn't care if he screws me,* or, *he hates Asian people, so he ran off.* Anything is possible. But it doesn't matter because he got away, and we are not gonna catch him and he is not going to have any bearing on my future.

So then, let's lean in the direction of giving people a break and try to give myself a positive experience! Also, then congratulate myself for a successful curation of my experience! Snaps to me! While I was not bouncing off the walls with excitement to be at the auto body shop, I felt good enough that I noticed the popcorn machine that was in the lobby. I asked the receptionist if I could have some and she said, "Sure."

"Can I have two bags?"

"Okay, but don't tell anyone."

We both laughed.

I scooped up two bags and announced, "Since the accident happened today, I am going to allow myself a cheat day in my intermittent-fasting diet."

Then the girl and I had a 15-minute discussion about diets, her children, her husband, and my comedy. I ended up making a new friend that day who would later show up to a comedy show that I was on! YAY!

Curating my emotions in the direction of positivity that day left me open for popcorn, a fun discussion, and making a new friend. I had every right to feel like a victim that day, but the victim mindset would not have left me open for other positive experiences.

In this chapter, Aidan stopped a negative emotional spiral!

In order to do this, you must understand the concept of emotional momentum!
Flash the QR code below for more info!

CONCLUSION

Over the last 8 chapters, I have described how to handle emotional emergencies. This is not to say that I don't have difficult moments. I've had bad dates, disappointments, and arguments that have definitely thrown me off-center. But in my active and deliberate curating of my story, I am much harder to knock off-center than I was. I am much more solid now in my emotional well-being than even before Michael passed.

The decision point of when I decided to stay alive and be happy was when I started prioritizing my emotional well-being instead of just managing conditions that I thought would bring me happiness. For example, starting a business in bubbles, producing comedy shows, making money, managing relationships, emulating successful people from Google who had never gone to college. Even my pursuit of academic competence and excellence in the performing arts all were strategies I was using to generate situations that I thought would bring me joy.

We all try to manage the world around us to create a positive feeling but I had never considered that I could actually manage the thoughts in my head to create that positive feeling. That we actually have the power to create

YAY from a visit to the Emergency Room, or strengthened your belief in yourself from a bad relationship, or a bad review from a respected comedy booker. We can, at every turn, choose to look at life from the perspective of optimism and hope and YAY!

Hopefully, the contents of this book has helped you feel a bit more empowered in caring for your emotions. Imagine that your emotional life is like living in a beautiful home that you love. Great, now you know how to deal with leaky roofs, exploding pipes, grease fires, and the occasional dog puke on the floor that you need to clean up. If you have an overflowing bathtub, you know how to go shut off the faucet instead of refusing to deal with the water by shoving a towel under the bathroom door, so you don't have to face the flood.

This is very important because unwanted situations will continue to arise as you move forward with life. Boy/girlfriends will come and go, surprising news will happen, your clothes will get ruined at the dry cleaners and the dogs will occasionally eat your homework! If you are sad, you won't just cover it up by stuffing your feelings with 12 bowls of ice cream. You might as well just get right to dealing with yourself emotionally.

As you start dealing with yourself from an emotional level you will find that your levels of happiness will rise as you start thinking creatively about how to meet your emotional needs. For example, if I am missing Michael because I would like a feeling of security, as long as I hold the position that Michael has to come back from the dead in order for me to get the security I will be without security. As you look at life from an emotional payoff standpoint you will feel more satisfied, empowered and joyful day to day.

As you feel yourself feeling better and better, you will notice that others around you will start to notice your positive attitude, and things in your life will go better for you. Why? It's not some voodoo law of attraction thing. It's because, very logically put, people want to be around happy strong people. Companies want to hire happy strong people. Potential mates are looking to make children with happy strong people. Everyone is looking to work with happy strong people. So be happy and strong, and you will be desired and valued.

Ironic then that your path to being happy and strong is actually valuing yourself enough to understand and meet your emotional needs.

The topic of emotional well-being is a topic that is so seldom addressed that if you were just keep yourself busy putting out emotional fires you would probably be doing pretty well in comparison to the majority of the nation. However! This book is called "The Art of Being Yay" not "The Art of Being Slightly More Okay Than Other People." So, now it's time to go the extra mile and apply the concepts covered in the previous chapters to increase your happiness thermometer.

What is a happiness thermometer? It's like if your home temperature is set to 45 degrees. No matter what the weather is like outside of your home, your central air conditioning system will work to keep your home at 45 degrees. It could be 20 degrees outside, or 120 but the A/C will continue to work to maintain your equilibrium. Likewise, all of us have a "Happiness Set Point." We can raise our go-to happiness level 1 degree at a time.

Take every chance you get and be deliberate about evidencing thoughts you think will aid you in the direction you would like to go! Be deliberate about them. Meet your emotional needs. Incrementally improve your opinion of yourself. Every thought, every moment you have a choice. Tick yourself up, or tick yourself down, as far as your emotional well-being. Keep ticking up. Miracles await.

FURTHER READING

The ideas contained in these books have changed my life.
I would recommend to anyone interested in strengthening
and conditioning their mindset for success and joy
to read the following. I've read each of these at least 4
times... (or listened to them on audible since I'm in traffic a
lot... I live in LA)

GRIT by Angela Duckworth
Angela Duckworth is a professor at University of
Pennsylvania who researches achievement and success.
According to Professor Duckworth, the number 1 indicator
for success in any field is not talent... turns out it's actually
the ability to stick it out! I have worn this book out! Anytime
I have a setback, I apply the concepts of this book to
leverage a motion forward. This book with give you tools
on how you can do that. It is a comforting, empowering and
beneficial if not downright necessary book.

MINDSET by Carol Dweck
Dr. Carol Dweck is a leading expert in motivation and
personality, and found that mindset creates our entire world.
Our mindset ultimately predict whether or not we will fulfill
out potentials. The mindset that you hold is everything, and

in this book she shares which mindset you can choose to hold in order to encourage your growth and success in any field. I can proudly say that I hold the key mindsets which allows me the faith that I can learn and improve in anything that I choose to put my focus on! Read this book!

THE HAPPINESS ADVANTAGE by Shawn Achor
Shawn Achor is a researcher at Harvard University who studies happiness and potential. The conventional wisdom is that one should go after goals, then when you hit the goals, then you achieve happiness. Turns out, this is backwards. Happiness first, then achievements follow. I mean... essentially this is what my book is about too right? It's true cause I lived it! But if you want more evidence because you like science and research, absolutely pick up this book. This book is one of the primary reasons why I put my happiness and well-being above anything else (i have not been perfect at this... remember Mel? YIKES haha!).

THE GOAL by Eliyahu M Goldratt, Jeff Cox
This is actually a business concepts book that served me very well and changed my life. It's written in a fiction story form about a guy who works as a factory plant manager, and it turns out that the factory is losing money because the over productiveness in parts of the plant which are creating problems in other aspects of the plant. Such a great lesson that working harder is not always the answer to a problem. It's about keeping your eye on "The Goal". Also, this book is fun because it has a definite 1980s Reagan Era feel to it (the wife at home with curlers, etc etc) I loved it and it shaped the way I think.

ASK AND IT IS GIVEN by Esther and Jerry Hicks
If you like the spiritual stuff. Nothing beats this. It's about using your power of focus to look in the direction of your desires versus focusing on which you don't want. Whether you believe in the Law of Attraction or not, the fact remains. If you continue to focus on that which you don't want, it is counterproductive. If you focus and move in the direction of what you want, you will be happier and what did we learn boys and girls? Happiness has a direct impact on your success in every which area of your life. So... read this book and pick up some tools that will aid you in being happier!

GET THE LIFE YOU WANT by Richard Bandler
Richard Bandler is a Co-Founder of NeuroLinguistic Programming which uses mental techniques to access the subconscious mind and reprogram your deeply held beliefs that hold you back. Remember, Carol Dweck proved that mindset is everything, so this book and list of techniques offered within it give you tools to deliberately choose which mindset you would like to encourage on the subconscious level.

ABOUT THE AUTHOR

Aidan Park is an author, speaker, empowerment coach, comedian and president of Solar Shark Inc. dedicated to spreading ideas and tools of empowerment and authentic joy! Combining his love for empowerment, comedy and teaching, Aidan has helped hundreds of individuals to personal breakthroughs by discovering their personal authentic joy and empowerment.

Because he could not pursue the traditional college education, Aidan became a student of empowerment and success principles which lead to his successes in multiple career fields. Aidan started his career as a musical theatre actor appearing in over 30+ theatre productiuons then successfully transitioned into on-camera in which he appeared in movies, TV, Commericals and other media projects.

Aidan soon became a comedian, producer and writer, organizing monthly live comedy shows at top comedy clubs in Hollywood including The Comedy Store, The Laugh Factory and The Hollywood Improv. Intent on raising awareness for the LGBT Community and HIV healthcare, Aidan often teamed up with organizations such as Aids

Healthcare Foundation, APLA, Equality California and No H8 Campaign in helping produce fundraising and awareness efforts to great success.

After the tragic loss of his partner Michael James in 2018, Aidan went on a journey to prioritize emotional well-being. What he learned impacted him in profound ways in dealing with his grief, that he decided to shift his career in the direction of empowering individuals to their personal authentic joy.

Aidan launched and founded Solar Shark Inc, through which he created a line of funny, educational and personal experience based products and launched a website AidanPark.com and TheArtofBeingYay.com featuring resources aimed at helping people care for their emotional health and feel less alone in the world.

Aidan practices what he preaches as he stays on his journey for deeper self-discovery and awareness. Aidan will only advocate tools and principles that he has personally tried for himself and that he has found works for him.

He lives in Los Angeles, CA.

STAY CONNECTED

Website: AidanPark.Com
Facebook: @Aidanparkshow
Instagram @Aidanparkshow
Email list/freebie: AidanPark.Com

Made in USA - Kendallville, IN
25447_9781649459497
12 09 2021 1752